D1383713

Columbia University

Contributions to Education

Teachers College Series

No. 727

AMS PRESS

NEW YORK

CHARACTERISTICS OF
GOOD AND POOR SPELLERS
A DIAGNOSTIC STUDY

BY DAVID HARRIS RUSSELL, Ph.D.

TEACHERS COLLEGE, COLUMBIA UNIVERSITY
CONTRIBUTIONS TO EDUCATION, NO. 727

Published with the Approval of
Professor Arthur I. Gates, Sponsor

BUREAU OF PUBLICATIONS
Teachers College, Columbia University
NEW YORK CITY
1937

Library of Congress Cataloging in Publication Data

Russell, David Harris, 1906-1965.
    Characteristics of good and poor spellers.

    Reprint of the 1937 ed., issued in series: Teachers
College, Columbia University. Contributions to educa-
tion, no. 727.
    Originally presented as the author's thesis, Colum-
bia.
    Bibliography: p.
    1. Spelling ability--Testing. 2. English language
--Orthography and spelling. I. Title. II. Series:
Columbia University. Teachers College. Contributions
to education, no. 727.
LB1574.R85 1972   372.6'32   73-177220

ISBN 0-404-55727-9

Reprinted by Special Arrangement with Teachers
College Press, New York, New York

From the edition of 1937, New York
First AMS edition published in 1972
Manufactured in the United States

AMS PRESS, INC.
NEW YORK, N. Y.   10003

ACKNOWLEDGMENTS

As SPONSOR of this study, Professor Arthur I. Gates has contributed the encouragement, the critical judgment, and the understanding guidance which made it possible. The work with him has been a pleasure and a privilege. Professors Carter Alexander, Ralph B. Spence, and Helen M. Walker also gave gladly of their assistance at various stages of the study's development.

The investigation would have been impossible without the kind co-operation of Mrs. Katherine Alfke of P. S. 43, Mrs. Harriet Hennessey of P. S. 125, and Mrs. Gertrude Talley of P. S. 165. Valuable assistance in collecting and tabulating the data was provided by workers of the Works Progress Administration Project 6063-C who included, particularly, Raymond Bunin, Morris Fischer, Andrew Halpin, Etta Karp, Edward Kelly, and Jacob Klein.

D.H.R.

CONTENTS

CHARACTERISTICS OF
GOOD AND POOR SPELLERS

A DIAGNOSTIC STUDY

CHAPTER I

THE PROBLEM

INTRODUCTION

THE MOST obvious spelling difficulties do not have equally obvious explanations. Any teacher knows *when* one of her pupils is a poor speller but seldom *why* he is. Her deficiency in the field is largely due to a general lack of knowledge of spelling. Despite a considerable number of careful studies, we still do not know how, in the process of learning to spell new words, certain basal factors cause a child to misspell. Our knowledge of the process of learning to spell and of factors underlying spelling disability is still too limited. This study aims to throw light on the relationships between the process of learning to spell, the kinds of responses made, and factors associated with incorrect responses.

The existing evidence on these relationships is summarized in Chapter II of this study. To give a complete report would necessitate drawing evidence from the contributions of physiology, neurology, and opthalmology, as well as experimental psychology in most of its branches. This would include a description of two general classes of investigation, the one utilizing instruments and laboratory techniques, the other individual and group tests of mental abilities, school achievement, and behavior in classroom activities, with occasional statistical analysis of results. While each of these divisions has made significant contributions, emphasis is placed on those studies most closely related to the learning situation in schools.

In a study of the process of learning to spell and of factors related to spelling disability, individual and group methods, and combinations of these, have been used. The combination of the two methods is used in this study; Gates has given the advantages of such a plan in a diagnostic study similar to the present one.

1

[28 : 2, 3]* The method of using groups has proved of value in such spelling studies as that of Carroll [12]; while the method seems sufficient to give constellations of factors associated with spelling difficulty, it often fails to explain the facts in an individual case. The present investigation considers whether spelling disability must become more and more a matter for individual study and a cause for individual teaching. Analysis of individual cases therefore becomes necessary. The method of the investigation, then, is to supplement the study of group differences between matched normal and retarded spellers with some further analysis of individual cases. This report is concerned with the process of learning to spell and the factors associated with spelling disability, interdependent terms which may require some explanation.

DEFINITION OF SPELLING DISABILITY

The term "disability" has been applied to cases of older school pupils who possess approximately zero ability in the spelling of words or in the learning of new words. Hollingworth says, "We find a few children of normal intellectual capacity whose spelling ability approaches zero" and "a few of the very extreme cases of disability will be unable to learn to spell, even with the maximum of effort." [40 : 96] But Hollingworth also states that "By far the greater proportion of the total sum of bad spelling is due to causes other than special disability—such as intellectual weakness, lack of interest, sensory defects, bad handwriting, etc." [40 : 74] It is necessary, then, to distinguish between "special disability" and "disability" in spelling. Gates expresses doubt as to the existence of special disability in the sense that a child, normal in most other respects, cannot be taught to spell correctly. [28 : 191-05]

It is the purpose of this report to deal with "disability" in the sense of retardation in spelling rather than with the concept of "special disability." Louttit suggests, "For practical purposes we may define a specific disability in spelling as an apparent inability to learn the spelling of words occurring among the two or three

* The number in brackets before the colon refers to a corresponding reference in the Bibliography; the numbers after the colon to pages in that reference.

thousand most frequently used." [47 : 212] The writer believes that this should be extended from the three or four thousand words commonly studied in the elementary school to include some special words needed and used by the child which are ordinarily not placed on such lists. Children are being studied in this investigation who are a year or more retarded in spelling. In general, spelling "disability" applies to those children who are so incapable of handling the common or special words, used by their peers and needed by themselves, that they are definitely hindered in the fluent expression of their ideas. Disability, as here used, does not imply that children are incapable of learning to spell, but means that they are, at the time, far below the norms for their respective grades and ages.

THE SPELLING PROCESS

The spelling process involves not only the formation of specific habits in the spelling of a certain number of words, say the three or four thousand most common; it includes also the technique for the learning of new words generally.

Most authorities agree that an adequate perceptual word attack and a memory for visual and auditory stimuli are fundamental aspects of the spelling process. The difficulty is that such a statement gives no real clue to the specific patterns involved in the process. Foran says, "Spelling is often regarded as merely memory and perception but such qualitative analyses or descriptions are little more than general observations which, even if correct quantitatively, do not reveal the parts played by the abilities that are identified. To determine the nature of spelling ability it is necessary to find its association with various factors and the extent to which these account for the whole performance." [22 : 190]

Pioneer writers as a rule failed to make this suggested analysis. For example, in 1892 Wyckoff said, "Knowledge of spelling begins with perception through eye and ear and ends with the establishment of a train of memories." We have "First, the sensation; second, the direction of attention; third, the retentiveness; fourth, the mental image; fifth, the automatic circuit." [72 : 448-49]

Such phrases as "train of memories" and "automatic circuit" are not clarified.

The first attempt to analyze the spelling process was made by Hollingworth in 1918. She divides the process of learning to spell a word into six steps:

1. Association of an object, act, quality, etc., with a certain sound.
2. Association of a sound or word with the highly complex muscular act necessary for articulating it.
3. The association of certain printed or written symbols with the objects, acts, etc., and with their vocal representations.
4. The association of separate symbols (letters) with each other in proper sequence for oral spelling.
5. The association of the visual perceptions of separate letters with the muscular movements of hand, arm, and fingers necessary to *copy* the word.
6. The association of the visual perceptions of separate letters with the motor responses necessary to produce the written word at pleasure. [40:79,80]

Hollingworth does not state how these associations may best be formed. The physiological bases suggested in the above are analyzed by Starch in a somewhat different fashion. Starch says,

The successive steps (in learning to spell) are substantially as follows:
1. The reading of the word, that is, the sight, sound, and pronunciation of the word as a whole which involves all the elements of the reading process . . .
2. Reception upon the retina (or the ear) of the visual (or auditory) stimuli of the first letter of the word.
3. Transmission of the visual (or auditory) impressions from the retina (or ear) to the visual (or auditory) centers of the brain.
4. Arousal thereby of mental images and other associations in learning.
5. Transmissions of the impulses from the visual (or auditory) centers to the motor-speech or to the motor-writing centers.
6. Transmission of motor impulses from the latter to the speech-organs or to the writing-muscles. This occurs very probably even in the silent reading of spelling since silent reading is accompanied by the so-called inner speech.
7. Execution of the speaking or writing movements in pronouncing or writing the letters.
8. Return kinaesthetic impulses from the speech or writing muscles to the sensory centers and then to the motor speech or writing centers. This series of steps from (2) to (8) is then repeated for the second letter, the third letter and so on to the end of the word.

Economy in learning to spell consists largely in providing conditions under which the half dozen links here outlined may be established most easily, most quickly, and most permanently for the words whose spelling the children should know. [62 : 374 ff.]

The value of such analyses as the above is questionable. Starch admits that we know little concerning the operation of the above factors or processes, and some of the physiological suggestions and the idea that the experienced speller sees only one letter at a time seem open to question. There seems to be little doubt that, while factors similar to these operate in all children's spelling, the individual responses differ to such an extent that generalization becomes difficult. However, such analyses indicate possible areas where disabilities may lie, particularly if the pedagogical rather than the physiological side is stressed.

Without knowing in detail all the organic factors involved in learning to spell, it is possible to state certain other factors which affect the spelling process and which are important from the point of view of the teacher or the individual learner. The process may be affected by:

1. The nature of the stimulus pattern.
2. The nature of the individual's receptors.
3. The nature of the individual's perceptual ability.
4. The ease of establishment of meaningful associations—relationships between letters and sounds, applications of certain generalizations, etc.
5. The student's motor ability—in speech and especially in writing.
6. The student's initiative and also his desire to perform effectively.

Studies of the spelling process have been made in each of these divisions. For example, when educators have disagreed as to whether presentation of words should be largely visual or largely auditory, they have considered the first of the above problems. Studies made in the teaching of homonyms are a part of the fourth division. It is by a study of such factors as the six given above that we contribute to the knowledge of how the process of learning to spell really operates. This study is not concerned with the first of these factors, treats the third somewhat incidentally, and aims to contribute to the other four.

LIMITATIONS AND PURPOSES OF THE STUDY

The present investigation does not pretend to study all the factors which might be causes of spelling disability or all factors involved in the spelling process. The relations between recognition and recall spelling are not included; accordingly auditory and visual memory spans are not studied. The study does not directly attempt to evaluate teaching methods except as they relate to specific auditory, visual, or speech factors. The eye movements in learning to spell new words are not studied by means of the ocular-photometer or similar apparatus.

In addition, the present study seeks to extend only incidentally our knowledge of visual perception as a factor in spelling ability. Studies by Gates, Sister Mary Irmina of the Visitation, Gates and Chase, and Horn all emphasize its importance. [25, 67, 31, 42] Pressey and others have emphasized the importance of "a good ear and a good memory for sounds" [55 : 204] but also stress the large part played by visual perception. The importance of visual perception in spelling is assumed, then, rather than investigated, in the present study.

By a method that combines the group and individual methods, this study attempts to throw light on such questions as the following:

1. What is the relation of spelling disability to
    a. Functional auditory factors such as auditory perception, acuity, and discrimination?
    b. Functional visual factors such as visual perception and acuity?
    c. Organic visual handicaps such as astigmatism and muscular imbalance?
2. To what extent is spelling disability associated with
    a. Speech handicaps such as bilingual background and mispronunciations?

b. Certain academic abilities such as silent reading, speed and quality of handwriting?

3. What are the most frequent types of spelling error made by each of the visual, auditory, and speech handicapped groups—omissions, transpositions, insertions, additions, phonetic, etc.?

4. How do the two groups of spellers (the normal and the retarded) differ in such factors as attitude toward spelling as a school subject, methods of studying new words in spelling, utilization of imagery, etc.?

SUMMARY

It is easy to observe difficulties in spelling but difficult to understand why they exist. The present study aims to throw light on the relationships between the process of learning to spell, the kinds of responses made in spelling, and the factors associated with incorrect responses. The method of the study is to compare group differences between individually matched normal and retarded spellers, supplemented by further analyses of individual cases of disability. Disability as used in the study does not imply that children are incapable of learning to spell but that they are so far below their grade standards that they are hampered in free expression and logical arrangement of their ideas. The spelling process is not defined as such, but six factors affecting it are stated—the nature of the stimulus pattern, the nature of the individual's receptors, the nature of his perceptual ability, the ease of establishment of meaningful associations, the individual's motor ability, and his initiative in learning.

CHAPTER II

REVIEW OF RELATED STUDIES

THE PROBLEMS OF SPELLING

SINCE spelling is a somewhat restricted field, the opinion is sometimes held that research has solved the problems in this more completely than in other subject-matter fields. This assumption is not borne out upon analysis of the problems involved. For example, on the basis of nearly one thousand cases of language difficulties, Orton says, "Spelling in our experience has been much more difficult of acquisition than reading and much more resistant to special retraining procedures. This can be readily understood when we appreciate that a much less mnemonic pattern is necessary for recognition than for recall." [53 : 165]

The school problems of spelling which are not entirely solved may be divided roughly into four divisions relating to:

1. The precise words to be taught.
2. The grade level at which these shall be presented.
3. The method of teaching the words.
4. The individual learner.

The study of "characteristics of good and poor spellers" comes, of course, under the fourth division.

It is beyond the scope of this report to summarize the research in the first two of these divisions, but it may be stated that careful work in these areas has left many problems still unsolved. [22 : 57] The present status of the third problem does affect the individual learner, with whom this study is concerned, and so may be summarized briefly.

PRESENT STATUS OF TEACHING METHOD

At present there seems to be rather general agreement as to the procedures employed in teaching spelling. That spelling must be

8

taught to the majority of our school population seems to be generally agreed. Gates found that a definite, planned method produced
better results than an "opportunistic" method of teaching. [23]
Horn states, "Rules cannot replace direct instruction in spelling,
even in the case of words covered by them." [42 : 55] Foran says,
"Children cannot learn the most effective methods by themselves
early enough to prevent the formation of any interfering habits."
[22 : 215] Schonell adds, "The incidental method of 'picking up'
spelling through other verbal activities does not work." [59 : 142]

Horn has suggested nine steps in studying a word which utilize
visual, auditory, and kinaesthetic clues and which are now in general use. [42 : 72] Gates has investigated the study-test and
test-study-test methods for the weekly spelling program. [24]
The latter is the plan in which the pupils are tested on the weekly
list at the beginning of the week, again at the end of the week, and
sometimes in midweek. Under this plan each pupil is to study
those words which he fails to spell correctly on any test. The
combination of the nine steps in studying a word as suggested by
Horn and the study-test or test-study plan as investigated by Gates
is now in rather general use.

This weekly program has been reinforced by the fact that many
recent spelling textbooks print lists of words (and sentences) to
be studied during one week under the above plans. These plans,
and the reduction of the words to be learned in elementary schools
to approximately four thousand, has undoubtedly meant more efficient spelling instruction. The course of study in spelling today
takes less time and probably produces better results than courses
employed at any time prior to about 1920.

There is a very real danger, however, that a set, ritualistic
method of teaching new words has become so widely adopted that
improvement in spelling teaching is being hindered. The view that
the last word has been said on spelling instruction is distinctly mis-
leading. The results of the present study indicate a need for
changes, and other recent studies have pointed out weaknesses in
the present system.

Thompson made a detailed investigation of the effects of a first class variety of the test-study plan of teaching spelling. He found that a pupil "half-learned" the words which were unknown to him on the pre-test. When a test was applied a few months after study, it was found that the pupil who originally failed on 50 per cent of the words now failed on 25 per cent; if he failed on 20 per cent of the words originally, he still failed on 10 per cent of them. The words were only "half-learned" under these relatively favorable conditions. [64]

Another study by Watson revealed that in high schools recruiting their pupils from one of the best city systems in the country, a large number of the freshmen were poor spellers. "Of the nineteen distributions, ten show less than 50 per cent reaching or exceeding the grade norm." [69 : 10] The evidence was clear that students advance through the elementary grades without having mastered an effective technique of learning how to spell new words. There seems to be little doubt that, by using diagnostic and remedial methods similar to those employed by Watson, an improvement in technique, in spelling conscience, and in general spelling ability could be consummated in the elementary school.

That steps in this direction are urgently needed has been revealed in the present study. In the preliminary testing the Modern School Achievement Test in spelling was given to 1185 children of grades 3, 4, and 5 in several New York City schools. These tests were prepared by a body of experienced testers on the basis of an analysis of curricula, and norms were established as a result of testing 6710 children in thirty-seven cities. [51] In the original testing done in the present study, of the 1185 children studied, 380 or 32.1 per cent were one year or more retarded in spelling. This result was obtained in schools where spelling is a regular part of the program. While the result is largely a function of the spread of ability in the classes tested (some retardation exists in all school subjects), this percentage of retardation in an above-average school system, together with the results of the studies mentioned, leads to the assumption that the optimum methods of spelling instruction are not being utilized.

When the best methods are not being employed it may mean

that teachers lack knowledge of the psychological problems involved in learning to spell and the causes of disability. This knowledge still needs to be discovered and verified. With the growth of diagnostic and remedial treatment in reading and other school subjects, the time seems ripe for an extension of these methods into the field of spelling. Horn has said that "The diagnosis and remedial treatment of spelling disabilities . . . offers one of the most fertile fields for further investigation." [41 : 145]

HISTORICAL BEGINNINGS

Some of the previous work in psychology and in spelling has contributed to this area. Two pioneer investigations which influenced the later history of diagnostic research in reading and spelling were made in early psychological laboratories. The first, the work of Javal in 1878, led to the use of modern apparatus for recording eye movements. [44] The second was the work of Cattell in 1885 upon the nature of perceptual reactions in reading. [13]

In 1892 Wyckoff tested poor spellers and emphasized perception through eye and ear and the establishment of a train of memories. [72] In 1901, in a study of the causes of chronic bad spelling, Carmen concluded that "Ability to spell well . . . probably implies not a *general* habit or power of observation, but a *special* ability to notice small differences in *words*." [11 : 89] In 1918 Hollingworth summarized these and other studies by saying, "All studies emphasize the fact that discrimination of sound and association of visual form with the sound of the word are main elements in spelling." [40 : 2]

In her own investigation, Hollingworth conducted a teaching and testing program in a class of fifteen pupils who were two years retarded in spelling but in not more than one other subject. Some of the conclusions were that disability is not necessarily a function of the quality of general intelligence, that ability to spell correctly is a complex process, that the most extreme cases of disability differ only in degree of defect from children in general, and that there is no one specific remedy for poor spelling. [40 : 100 ff.]

Shortly after this report the number of investigations in spelling grew rapidly and results of different studies may best be considered in certain rough categories. For purposes of showing results the studies may be divided into the following arbitrary (and not necessarily discrete) divisions:

1. Studies dealing with constitutional factors—intelligence, sensory apparatus, imagery, etc.
2. Studies dealing with related scholastic abilities—reading, handwriting, and speech.
3. Studies dealing with specific techniques in learning to spell—eye movements, syllabication, etc.
4. Studies dealing with other factors such as attitudes, personality difficulties, etc.
5. Miscellaneous studies involving several factors.

These divisions are summarized in order in the section following.

CONSTITUTIONAL FACTORS

Intelligence. Most investigators agree that constitutional factors may play an important role in spelling disability. While spelling is not so closely related to intelligence as is reading, some relationship does exist. Results of several studies are summarized in Table I.

TABLE I

Investigations Showing Correlation between Spelling and Intelligence

Date	Investigator	No. of Cases	Grades	r (Intelligence and Spelling)
1915	Houser (43)..........	186	4 to 8	.53
1918	Hollingworth (40)....	15	5	.31
1919	Murray.............		College	.42
1922	Gates (28)..........	105	3 to 8	.31
1926	Gates (25)..........	234	3 to 7	.41
1935	Watson (68).........	"Insufficient"	9	.23
1936	Schonell (59)........	82 men	18–22 yrs.	.19
1936	Schonell (59)........	249	9–14 yrs.	.55 (verbal group test)

These coefficients of correlation are not so large as those between intelligence and reading, but it would seem that low mental ability may affect spelling ability within certain restricted limits. Horn states this in one way, "The poorer showing which . . . children of inferior intelligence have made has been due, in part, to inferior methods of learning" [42 : 64], which in turn are related to mental ability.

Sensory Disabilities. More important than low mental ability as a cause of disability would seem to be other constitutional factors such as organic defects, and functional sensory disabilities such as visual and auditory perception, due to organic difficulties and lack of training. A review of the literature indicates that outstanding organic defects are rare, but when they occur are often a major cause of disability. This seems to be less true of deafness than of visual, speech, or kinaesthetic difficulties. Gates and Chase found that in comparison with normal children of the same reading ability the deaf children were superior by three or four years. At the same time, however, the deaf were retarded in spelling on an average of nearly three years in the junior high school grades. [31]

Of what may be considered another type of constitutional defect, Selzer believes that retardation in reading, writing, spelling, and speech may be "due to disturbance of lateral dominance in the cerebrum." [61] The only other writer to support this view seems to be Orton, who says, "Apparently in the normal literate adult there is an intimate interweaving between such fractions of the language faculty as reading, writing, spelling and speaking, which results in considerable overlapping, so that the results of even the most restricted brain damage are apt to be complex and rarely if ever do we see pure syndromes such as can be demonstrated in some of the developmental disorders of children." [53 : 144]

As well as organic defects, the functional sensory abilities have received considerable attention. As stated above, the importance of visual perception has been stressed by all investigators in that area.

Gates summarizes: "1. Correlations show that word-perception is an important factor in the determination of success in spelling ($r = .55$) 2. The most common cause of misspelling is to be found in inadequacy of acquaintance with the visual form of the word." [28 : 86] Both Gates and Sister Visitation emphasize perceptual discrimination such as the ability to see similarities and differences in groups of letters and words (but not in numbers or geometric designs) as an important part of visual perception. "Of the several abilities studied, that termed 'word-perception' is most closely associated with achievement in reading and spelling." [25 : 444] Gates and Chase believe that the deaf owe their remarkable spelling ability primarily to a particularly effective type of perceiving words visually. [31]

Gilbert had considerable success teaching spelling by means of flash cards which, of course, place a premium on speed and accuracy of visual perception. [33]

Hartmann gave eight individual tests of auditory and visual capacities to groups of good, average, and poor spellers among college freshmen. He found that the test which best distinguished the groups was one of "perceptual span for meaningful material" consisting of one second exposure of twenty hard words in a tachistoscope, later mixed with "confusion stimuli" in the form of other words. Hartmann concludes, "Good spellers perceive total configurations of the verbal sort with greater facility than others. Secondly, spelling ability is essentially a central function; with normal subjects peripheral factors of an optical or retinal nature are inconsequential." [36 : 698] As a result of his experiment Hartmann suggests the possibility of using the meaningful perceptual span as a determiner of spelling talent.

These and other studies indicate the importance of visual perception, particularly of verbal forms, as a necessary part of the equipment of all good spellers. The emphasis seems to be upon the perception of the word, not upon the memory of it. Foran says, "The perceptual nature of spelling places the emphasis on seeing words, noting similarities between them and other words, writing them . . . While memorization is needed, spelling cannot be successfully taught merely by having the children spell the words aloud frequently without writing them or seeing them. The emphasis must always be placed on the apprehension of the word." [22 : 199]

An application of perception was found by Hansburg in a series of experiments to determine the effect of work in a print shop upon spelling. The first experiments show that work in printing definitely improves spelling, a reliable difference in improvement being found on various numbers of words studied and paragraphs set up. By comparing the gains of printing, studying, and control groups, a second type of experiment showed that improvement was not the result of mere practice in reading over and memorizing the material used for the typesetting. "Apparently practice in reading and studying the material is not alone responsible for the improvement made by the typesetting group in spelling. The other processes involved in printing, namely, typesetting, proofreading, the critical examination of words during correction and resetting, seem to be the procedures responsible for the spelling improvement. In other words, the very processes peculiar to the printing activity are the significant factors." [35 : 101] Further results showed that the spelling improvement occurred when the regular curriculum or specially prepared exercises were used as copy for typesetting; there was some tendency for spelling transfer to closely related words, and spelling improvement seemed to be permanent.

Imagery. Under the general heading of constitutional factors has been placed "imagery." Different writers have stressed the importance of "imagery" from time to time, but there seems to be little agreement as to its existence or its importance. Carney states that "The discovery of the precise image type of an individual constitutes a very difficult and elusive problem." [10 : 71]

In a summary of principles of help in teaching spelling Sudweeks gives eleven references for the statement: "13. People differ in the effectiveness of the four types of learning (visual, auditory, hand-motor, and speech-motor) in application to spelling." [63 : 109] In a somewhat similar summary Horn states, "Most people use readily two or more types of imagery, shifting unconsciously from one to the other; often for no discoverable reason." [42 : 71] He states that the difference is slight whether the most favorable or the directly opposite type of imagery is used. It is generally agreed that children cannot be divided into discrete types on the basis of the dominancy of any particular kind of imagery, and, furthermore, that there is little or no relationship between ability in sensory perception and vividness of imagery. Auditory imagery, in the form of dependence on the sound of a word, may prove a spelling handicap in a language as unphonetic as English, but it seems probable that a vivid visual imagery (if such exists) may aid a child in forming a mental picture of words that will be an asset in spelling. Sudweeks gives ten references in support of the rule "14. Appeal to the student through as many senses and types of imagery as possible; and, if a particular type of imagery is found especially effective with a student, make special use of that type with him." [63 : 110] For practical purposes it may be more important to discover the method of study, rather than the precise imagery, which is most effective.

Scholastic Abilities

But spelling ability probably depends on factors other than constitutional ones. Imagery is uncertain at best and Sister Visitation has shown that intelligence and accuracy of visual perception, while very significant, are not the sole factors in spelling ability. She used partial correlation techniques between reading and spelling; with intelligence and several verbal perception tests partialled out the zero order coefficients were reduced by almost one-half. The residual coefficients were, however, between .30 and .50 [67:41] indicating that there are other factors in addition to intelligence and visual perception involved in reading and spelling. Some of these factors may be included in other academic abilities. Abilities related to spelling may be found in reading, handwriting, and speech, among others.

Reading. It has already been indicated that reading and spelling share dependence on perceptual ability. "The data support the hypothesis that much of the connection between ability in reading and ability in spelling is due to the dependence of each on the capacity to observe small similarities and differences between word forms." [22 : 195] There are few results available, however, on the relation of spelling to ability in reading for different purposes. In spelling the one main purpose is to reproduce a word correctly so that all may recognize it. In reading the purpose may be skimming to get the main idea of a selection, reading to get an experience of continuity of facts or events, or reading to note details in difficult technical material. It is found that children who are skilled in one type are not necessarily competent in another, but we have little information on how skill in the different kinds of reading affects spelling ability.

Furthermore, the so-called good reader may not necessarily be a good speller. Hilderbrandt recognizes that "Occasionally one finds a good reader who is a poor speller. It seems that his ability to perceive a word, though satisfactory for reading, is not sufficiently precise to assist much in spelling. Yet when specific, favorable reactions have been set up in the spelling of a word, reading tends to preserve them." [38 : 373]

Not only may the type of skill in reading affect spelling but the way reading is learned may have some influence. The once popular phonetic method of teaching reading (as an exclusive method) has been attacked on the grounds of its effect on spelling. Hilderbrandt says, "The phonetic method of teaching reading is not most highly conducive to the development of spelling ability, though it tends to promote the method of spelling by sound. Sometimes the individual lays too much stress on phonetic elements. He treats them as units, and so obstructs his view of the word as a group of significant parts or as a whole." [38 : 374]

Horn states that "Children who learn by a phonic method seem to have no advantage in learning to spell." [42 : 63] The fact that they are a little more certain on initial letters and vowels is offset by the tendency to leave out silent letters and to insert letters. "Letter methods involving word-building are apt to cause children to invert word-forms. . . . The sentence method of teaching reading produces, in a much shorter time, a spelling efficiency at least equal to that produced by synthetic methods, in equal times, a greater efficiency." [34 : 315]

The question of method in reading and spelling (see Chapter VII) has not been sufficiently studied from the standpoint of relationships in the two subjects to give any clear statement. The effect of methods in reading only, in relation to auditory and visual characteristics of pupils, has been studied by Bond [6] and by Fendrick [18] who find that an exclusively auditory or visual method will handicap those pupils who have auditory or visual defects, respectively.

It may be possible that one of the reasons for the present retardation in spelling ability, as determined in some of the initial testing in this study, may be the decline in word study by means of phonic or other methods. Other writers have suggested word analysis methods as an aid to spelling. The phonetic method as such may be of little use in a language that has the same sound in many combinations of letters such as in no, low, owe, sew, four, beau, dough, and chauffeur; or in a language in which one letter gives different sounds such as "a" in ate, at, arm, path, care, tail, and what. At the same time, phonetic analysis does call attention to particular parts of words, whereas many modern reading methods emphasize using the whole word or phrase. It is a possibility that the habit of attention to word-parts may transfer from a phonetic method.

Handwriting. It is generally agreed that handwriting affects spelling ability, particularly in the written test situation. In addition to the obvious effect of letters so shaped that they are confused with others, there may be some patterns of motor facility involved. Hilderbrandt says, "Spelling links itself with writing even more closely than with reading . . . (The pupil's) ability to spell is based partly on associations that he has built up between movements, and partly on associations established between elements of perception. It is not unusual for a person who is uncertain of the spelling of a word to write it, or at least to go through the motions of writing it, before he uses it, in order to make sure that his spelling is correct." [38 : 374]

With the emphasis on diagnostic procedures in the present study, a recent report on handwriting by Cole is pertinent. The study involved 85 control and 92 experimental children in grades 2, 3, and 4. The experimental group were given exercises, each of which presented only one new word and was concerned with the practice of only one new letter. The conclusions stress the importance of diagnosis and individual remedial work instead of the general drill usually given. "Children's main defects of handwriting are due to particular mistakes on particular letters . . . only diagnosis will reveal the defects, only self-analysis will convince the pupil, and only individualized drill will provide a remedy." [14 :- 221] Such a statement applies in the spelling situation to the case of the child whose unclosed "a's" look like "u's," whose uncrossed "t's" look like "l's," etc.

Handwriting errors have been discussed from another point of view. Hollingworth says that errors in spelling may be due to motor awkwardness and inco-ordination, and to lapses which are spontaneous and for the most part unconscious. [39] After an experiment in speeded-up writing, Roback concluded that "Nearly all the lapses and deviations of the handwriting are due, according to our theory, to two complementary processes in the nervous system, viz., *perseveration* and *assimilation*, the first referring to the tendency of a movement to be repeated, whether in substitution of another or superfluously; the second process relating to the tendency of one movement to resemble another in close proximity and in accordance with certain cues which would favor such assimilation." [58 : 138] Roback also discusses the role of the unconscious in writing lapses.

Speech. Speech has been much less of a school subject than reading or writing, until comparatively recent times, because schools stressed only formal aspects of language. The more modern programs have made a beginning in emphasizing correct pronunciation and rhythm, the correction of speech defects, and the importance of a background of ideas for speech. Authorities agree that correct speech is important for spelling. Sudweeks gives three references in support of the statement that "The importance of correct pronunciation as an aid to spelling is great; teachers and pupils should take care to pronounce words clearly and distinctly." [63 : 114]

From two experiments with university students Kiefer and Sangren conclude that "Poor enunciation was typical of most of the poor spellers." [46 : 42]

Foreign language spoken in the home may affect a child's spelling scores. Horn says, "The average for children of foreign parentage may be expected to be slightly less than for children of native parentage." [42 : 63] The opinion is held that errors in spelling are just as common in phonetic languages such as Spanish and German as they are in non-phonetic languages. It seems probable that for a pupil who has been taught in these or other phonetically spelled languages, the difficulty of spelling English, with its many non-phonetic forms, may be increased.

Of a study of the effect of pronunciation training on spelling in the fifth and sixth grades, Kay concludes from rather inadequate evidence, "Forty-eight of the fifty children taking part in the experiment corrected both the pronunciation and spelling of some words and twelve of them corrected both spelling and pronunciation of five or more words. From these results, the conclusion is that the study of pronunciation is helpful in the correction of spelling." [45 : 66]

The chief investigation of the effects of speech defects has been done by Schonell. From 7000 London pupils he selected for study 105 elementary pupils who were backward in spelling (and in some cases reading). The percentage of serious speech defects in the group was about 16 per cent; in the backward group 7.3 per cent of the boys had an intense functional defect.

Schonell concludes that "paraphemia is the condition which most affects attainments in reading and spelling. In the current investigation it proved to be a major causal factor in the disability of four boys." [60 : 129] This supports a former statement that organic defects, while rare, may be a major cause of disability. "Intense functional paraphemia was the speech defect which was the most potent cause of disability in spelling." [60: 137]

There remain the much greater number of pupils who make constant mistakes in pronunciation and enunciation. Of these Schonell says,

The extreme verbal retardation of all these cases demonstrates one point, namely, the importance of articulatory—auditory process in learning to spell and to read. If either through organic defects in the necessary organs or through an initial weakness in discrimination of "letter sounds" (which unless there is extra training of a systematic type leads to fixation of faulty speech habits) children are unable to speak correctly they labor under a handicap which in acquirement of skill in reading and spelling is often greater than that occasioned by defective vision. [60:133]

Throughout the present investigation there was ample evidence that faulty pronunciation was a prolific contributory cause of misspelling. Naturally it was never the major or sole causal factor in a case of backwardness, but it was observed that if a child constantly pronounced inaccurately he not infrequently spelt inaccurately and the nature of his written errors bore remarkable similarity to the nature of his spoken errors." [60:136]

Schonell does not give enough specific data in his report to allow the reader to verify this close relationship between speech errors and spelling errors. Mendenhall has pointed out that over fifty per cent of spelling errors are "reasonably phonetic." [50 : 53] (He considers "parck" for "park" and "arond" for "around," etc., as reasonably phonetic errors, misspellings which would be classified as an insertion and an omission in the present study.) The high percentage of "reasonably phonetic" errors lends some support to Schonell's observation of the close relationship between speech and spelling errors, but further evidence is required to determine exact relationships.

SPECIFIC TECHNIQUES IN LEARNING NEW WORDS

It is usually given as one of the aims of spelling that children not only learn to spell a certain fixed number of words but learn how to study new words with the idea of mastering them. Foran says, "A technique for the learning of new words is as important as the specific habits formed for the spelling of common words." [22 : 3] Also it would seem that the method by which a word is learned has much to do with the accuracy of its recall at some later date. For these two reasons, at least, it would seem that the method of learning to spell is important. Research has investigated method in the larger sense such as the test-study and study-test programs [24] or column and context methods of teaching [49] but has little reliable evidence on how individual techniques should be employed. The work of Lay [8] and of Baird [56] suggest a method combining several methods of presentation but "the evidence employed to prove the worth of this principle is of questionable validity." [22 : 82]

Winch found contradictory results in the use of "a visual, motor-articulatory and auditory method" in comparison with an "exclusively visual method" in two schools, one of boys, and one of girls of somewhat higher mental ability. [70 : 71]

Despite the lack of objective evidence, however, schools have widely adopted plans of presenting words similar to that suggested by Horn. [42 : 72] This plan suggests nine steps in the study of a word, such as saying the word, closing the eyes to recall how it looks, writing the word without looking at the book, etc. It may be that using all these steps with every pupil is a wasteful procedure; some pupils may find it necessary only to write a word saying the letters in syllables, another only to visualize the word correctly a few times. It may be that a combination of visual, auditory, and kinaesthetic stimuli is needlessly complex for many students. It is hoped that the conclusions of the present study throw more light on the process of the *individual* employing these different steps.

Most workers agree that "saying the letters does not add to efficiency" and it has been found to be the method used by poor spellers. [1 : 16] Correct pronunciation, understanding the meaning of the words, and syllabication are considered an aid to correct spelling. In general, it is agreed with Horn that "The methods which are suitable for the good speller are apparently also suitable for the poor speller" [42 : 64], but the precise techniques which are best for the individual speller cannot be stated without study of that individual.

The methods of studying words has been investigated from another viewpoint by Gilbert [32] and by Abernethy [2]. They studied the relationship between efficiency in learning and the method of learning to spell as indicated by photographic records of eye movements. Both investigators found that the method used was repeated surveys of the word with regressions at difficult parts. Adults and superior spellers study by syllables but make a detailed analysis of especially difficult parts of a word. Abernethy states that, at the sixth grade level, good and poor spellers "differ mainly in the more marked tendency of the good spellers to recognize difficulties and to make a systematic attack in studying words" and concludes that "Analysis of eye-movements probably needs to be supplemented by a more subjective method of analysis." [2 : 701] Such a method is attempted in the present study.

OTHER FACTORS

The technique of presenting words is not the whole teaching of spelling; the provisions for meeting the everyday needs of the pupil, the direction of study activities, and the pupil's reaction to them, may have greater effect on learning. It seems that a general attitude toward the school situation, or other "personality" traits, may include and affect the spelling lesson.

Kiefer and Sangren measured non-intellectual traits by means of the Will-Profile Test of the Carnegie Institute of Technology. They found that "perseveration" (characterized by continuous effort to attain an indefinitely defined end), "speed of decision," and "freedom from inertia" are all associated with good spellers on the college level.

Blanchard suggests that, with diagnostic methods and remedial teaching methods prevalent in schools more than formerly, children referred to clinics are now often "burdened with emotional conflicts that made response to teaching impossible and indicated the need of therapy." [5 : 394] She says, "Reading disabilities very clearly in many instances are a part of a more general difficulty in achieving normal emotional growth." [5 : 397] Fendrick and Bond have shown that reading disability and delinquency are associated. [19] What is true of reading may apply (in less degree) to other school subjects, including spelling. There may be a tendency for parents to emphasize a child's difficulty as primarily educational rather than one which involves the home situation, but the causal relationships of failure in school subjects and general emotional maladjustment have not been made clear. Certainly the literature contains many case studies of pupils who by achieving success in one or more of the school subjects apparently became better adjusted to their school and community environment.

In a study of the causes of spelling disability among educated adults, Schonell, as well as attributing disability to sensory defects and weak perception, gives the following causes:

Temperamental—1. General emotional instability
             2. General disregard for details
             3. Inferiority attitude toward spelling disability
             4. Apathy with regard to disability

Environmental— 1. Early absence from and continued change of school. [59:133]

In a list of twelve possible causes of poor spelling Hollingworth lists items which include personality factors. These include lapses, transfer of habits previously acquired, such as from a phonetic language, idiosyncrasies such as adding a final "e" to all words, and temperamental traits such as indifference, carelessness, lack of motivation, and distaste for intellectual drudgery.

In this section are included a few studies which involved the discovery of various characteristics, some of which have been mentioned above. A study by Ile confirmed a previous one by Floyd which gave the major causes of spelling disability in twenty-six cases studied as: defective vision 2, defective hearing 1, speech defect 1, inferior learning capacity 5, poor observation 3, poor visual memory 2, poor auditory memory 2, immaturity 2, lack of interest 4, lack of acquaintance with the English language 1, writing difficulty 2, lack of training 1. [57 : 284]

As the result of a survey of a city school system, Davis found 275 pupils in grades 2 through 6 who were in need of remedial work. The most common difficulties were: [15]

1. Has not mastered steps in learning to spell a word   88
2. Writes poorly   88
3. Cannot pronounce the words being studied   78
4. Has bad attitude (a) application, (b) lack of interest   71
5. Does not associate the sound of the letters or syllables with the spelling of a word   49

8. Has speech defect   16
13. Has poor hearing   5
16. Has poor vision   3

McGovney gave a series of tests to fourteen poor spellers of superior general ability. They were below standard in handwriting, in supplying phonetic equivalents of letters, in perceiving small differences between words, in remembering visual symbols, and in associating the spoken word with word-like symbols. [48]

As a result of an extensive testing program on 135 pupils of one school and other individual cases of reading and spelling disability, Gates concludes that "The causal factors which seemed probable or possible (are) . . . A. Unfavorable Training and Environmental Factors. B. Unfavorable Behavior of a General Character. C. Defects of the Sensory Mechanisms. D. Defects of the Motor Mechanisms. E. Defects of the Connecting Mechanisms." [28 : 89]

Among miscellaneous factors might be listed the possibility of a general linguistic ability which has been suggested by Traxler and others. Traxler says, "There are, however, a number of factors that tend to complicate the problem of diagnosis and remedial teaching of spelling. One is that spelling ability seems to be a part of a larger, more general language ability and that excessive difficulty with spelling is often correlated with great learning handicaps in oral speech, written language usage, and reading." [67 : 35]

Such studies as those above impress the fact that the diagnostician or remedial teacher can look for no one cause of spelling disability. This is not to be understood as an insuperable difficulty. Since only a fraction of the school population have real difficulty with spelling, and as diagnostic methods improve, it seems possible for the classroom teacher to apply some objective diagnostic tests to the particular pupils who need the help. With more complete understanding of some of the major and minor causes of disability suggested in the studies summarized above, we can hope for schools in which nearly one-third of the pupils are not handicapped by spelling disability.

Summary

Spelling problems fall into four main divisions; the present study touches on two of them: (1) methods of teaching and (2) the individual learner. There is today rather general agreement as to a teaching method; the varieties of this generally accepted method are perhaps too inflexible in light of modern needs. Thompson and Watson have shown that spelling instruction is still inefficient. Other investigations into factors associated with the individual learner are summarized under: constitutional factors; scholastic achievements—reading, handwriting, and speech; specific techniques in learning new words; personality factors; and studies involving miscellaneous factors. Different investigations emphasize different conditions or combinations of conditions in the above areas and their subdivisions as the causes of spelling disability. Spelling disability rarely seems to be associated with only one or with all the above factors, so individual diagnosis is usually required.

CHAPTER III

PROCEDURE

CLASSIFICATION OF CHILDREN USED AS SUBJECTS

THE CASES making up the sixty-nine individually matched pairs of the present study were selected from among the children of four New York public schools. The children were pupils in grades 3, 4, and 5 (both sections A and B) in Public Schools 43, 125, 165, and 500. The schools are characterized by splendid co-operation for experimental purposes, accessibility to Teachers College for testing purposes, and a range of neighborhood from rather poor to good. The pupil population of two of the schools is somewhat below average for the city, a third is above average, and the fourth is an experimental school.

In the above grades the Modern School Achievement Test in Spelling was administered. This test consists of writing words in spaces provided in sentences printed on the test blank. The test was constructed of words in common use which are of such a form that they provide opportunities for diagnosis in some of the commonest types of spelling errors. Norms are available on these words as a result of testing 6710 children in thirty-seven cities. [51] In the present study the test was given to 1185 children in the above grades and schools, who were then each assigned a grade score in spelling.

On these pupils, data were obtained from the official school records regarding chronological age and amount of schooling. The records were not verified otherwise as they were considered sufficiently exact for comparative purposes in the experiment. For each pupil was available, then, sex, chronological age, school attended, grade status, number of terms (half-years) in school, and spelling grade. In addition, intelligence quotients were available for the pupils in three schools obtained from the Stanford-Binet

27

Intelligence Examination by examiners known to the writer. In the fourth school, some group intelligence test results were available. In this school additional National Intelligence Examinations were given where no result was available. Where conflicting results had been recorded a Stanford-Binet Intelligence Examination was administered.

The above records, including intelligence quotient, were completed for practically all of the 1185 pupils. Then the pupils who were one year or more retarded in spelling grade and also the normal or better spellers for their grade were selected. Individuals in these two groups were then matched as to sex, school attended, grade, chronological age, intelligence quotient, and terms in schools. The maximum variation allowed was six months in chronological age, five points in intelligent quotient, and one term in school, with the exception of grade 5B where a spread of two terms was allowed. That the matching was rigid was evidenced in that only 69 matched pairs were obtained from the 1185 pupils. Of these, 61 pairs were given the complete list of eighteen tests, and sufficient results were obtained in the case of the 8 other pairs to include them in most of the calculations.

The subjects in the experiment, then, composed two groups matched individually as to sex, chronological age, intelligence quotient, grade, terms in school, and varying only in spelling grade. The one group were normal or better spellers for their grade, the others were at least one year retarded in spelling. For each matched pair the minimum difference in spelling grade was one year and, in some cases, ran as high as three years.

COMPARISON OF QUALIFYING CASES

For purposes of convenience, only aggregate information is given regarding the data utilized in matching the 138 cases (69 pairs). Table 2 is a condensation of these data to illustrate the similarities and differences of the two major groups of the study.

Table 2 reveals that the mean I.Q. of the normal spelling group is about one point above that of the retarded group, that the retarded group on the average has attended school one and one-third

TABLE 2*

Comparison of Matching Data for Normal and Retarded Spelling Groups
(N = 69 each group)

	Normal (x)		Retarded (y)		D	r_{xy}	σ_D	C.R.$_\sigma$
	Mean	S.D.	Mean	S.D.	$M_x - M_y$			
1. Intelligence quotient.......	102.65	11.71	101.52	11.19	1.13	.940	0.48	2.35
2. Terms in school...	7.32	1.83	7.59	2.03	0.27	.957	0.08	3.38
3. Chronological age (months)......	115.86	13.67	115.48	13.59	0.38	.961	0.46	0.83
4. Spelling grade....	5.05	0.88	3.02	0.81	2.03	.754	0.07	29.00

* The formulas used in this table and in similar tables throughout this report were:

$$1. \quad \sigma_D = \sqrt{\frac{\sigma^2_x + \sigma^2_y - 2r_{xy}\,\sigma_x\,\sigma_y}{N-1}}$$

$$2. \quad C.R._\sigma = \frac{D}{\sigma_D}$$

months longer than the normal group, and that the mean difference in chronological ages is about one-third of a month. The smallness of these differences is emphasized in view of the large critical ratios obtained. The formulas used (see table footnote) mean that as the coefficient of correlation (r_{xy}) increases, the standard error (σ_d) of the differences decreases and accordingly the critical ratio increases. Here the coefficients of correlation equal about .95; they are so high that they increase the critical ratios to values which do not show a true picture of the matching involved. On item 4, the difference of over two years in spelling grade and a critical ratio of 29.0 is to be expected since the groups were so matched that each normal speller was at least one year in advance of his retarded match.

TESTS USED

In addition to the Modern School Achievement Test in Spelling, and the intelligence examinations, used for grouping, each pupil of the 69 pairs was given the following tests: [1]

[1] As noted above, due to circumstances beyond the control of the examiners, tests were not entirely completed on eight pairs. The numbers have been omitted in the proper summaries of results.

   I.   Handwriting Test—Speed
   II.   Handwriting Test—Quality
  III.   Battery of Nine Diagnostic Tests related to Spelling Abilities
  IV.   Test of Auditory Acuity
   V.   Betts Visual Sensation and Perception Tests
  VI.   Speech Schedule and Recording
 VII.   Gates Silent Reading Tests (Grades 3 to 8), Types A and D

A brief description of the various tests is given in the following paragraphs.

I. *Handwriting—Speed*

For the speed test in handwriting the subjects were asked to write the words "Mary had a little lamb" as often as they could in three minutes' time. The scores were computed in terms of letters per minute.

II. *Handwriting—Quality*

For the test of quality in handwriting the Thorndike Handwriting Scale was used. For this measure the pupils are asked to write a prescribed paragraph in their best handwriting. The complete instructions for administering the test and scoring the handwriting are given on the Scale. [65] The handwriting samples were rated by five judges and an average was taken. The results and reliability of the judging are given in Chapter V.

III. *Battery of Diagnostic Tests Related to Spelling Abilities*

This battery comprises nine tests, six of which are based on the Gates Diagnostic Series in reading as given in the 1927 and the 1935 editions of "The Improvement of Reading." [27] A copy of the blank on which the results were recorded is given in Appendix C. The sub-tests are as follows:

1. *Spelling Words Orally* (Gates Test B 4). The subject is asked to pronounce after the examiner and spell orally 36 given words. The methods of spelling (hesitations, letter by letter, by syllables, phonetically, etc.) are recorded up to a total of ten errors. These errors are analyzed as to additions, insertions, omissions, substitutions, transpositions, and phonetic spelling, on the blank provided.

2. *Word Pronunciation Test* (Gates Test VII 1). The pupil is asked to read and pronounce fifty words (the alternate items on the Gates test). His methods of attack on unfamiliar words (use of phonetics, blending, etc.) and pronunciation errors (omissions, transpositions, etc.) are recorded.

3. *Giving Letters for Letter Sounds* (Gates B 1). The examiner gives the commonest sound for ten letters and asks the subject to name the letter.

4. *Spelling One Syllable* (Gates B 2). The subject is asked to pronounce after the examiner and spell ten nonsense words of one syllable each, for example, ub, ip.

5. *Spelling Two Syllables* (Gates Test B 3). The subject is asked to pronounce after the examiner and spell eight nonsense words of two syllables each, for example, nubit, argos. Some of these words repeat (in combination) syllables of test 4.

6. *Reversals* (Gates Test VIII 1). The pupil is asked to read quickly thirty words which are subject to complete or partial reversals by certain readers, for example, reading no for on, rats for star.

7. *Spelling Attack.* Of the ten words which were incorrect on Test 1, the four hardest words (the seventh, eighth, ninth, and tenth errors) were selected for further study by the subject. These words are presented one at a time to the pupil on typewritten cards. He is asked to study the words just as he usually studies words in spelling and so as to be sure to have them correct when he writes the four words later. The pupil is encouraged to think aloud (for purposes of recording his responses). His methods of studying the hard word, such as closing eyes to recall appearance, writing the word, spelling orally letter by letter, etc., are recorded, as well as the length of time spent on each word. Fifteen devices used in word study may be recorded on the blanks used.

8. *Auditory Discrimination.* A jumbled list of pairs of words which sound alike is presented to the subject to test whether or not he can recognize (pronounce) each word. When the examiner is satisfied that the subject knows all the words the latter is given a test blank in which the words of similar sounds are paired, such as

be-by, do-to, etc. The examiner then stands approximately six feet behind the pupil and reads one of each pair while the pupil underlines the word he thinks the examiner said. The score is the number of words correctly underlined.

9. *Visual, Auditory, and Kinaesthetic Methods of Studying Words*. The purpose of this test is to discover, if possible, any differences existing between the subjects in the ease and accuracy with which they utilize the above three methods of studying hard words. Three words were studied by each of the so-called auditory, visual, and kinaesthetic methods.

The words studied by each method were of the same number of letters and approximately equal difficulty. They were obtained by matching the words of Test 1 with two other words on the Buckingham-Dolch "Combined Word List." [9] The words of Test 1 were matched with other words from the combined list by the following considerations:

1. Words with same number of letters.
2. The words selected as close as possible to the original word in the Payne-Garrison Spellers in which "words were assigned to various grades in terms of their frequency and difficulty—as determined by an intensive investigation."
3. Words agreed on placement in at least three out of five of "Horn Vocabulary of Six Year Olds," "Kindergarten Union List," "Jones List," "Tidyman Speller," "Thorndike Word Book." (On the harder words the first two lists were replaced by the Buckingham-Dolch list.)

The three lists of words [2] thus obtained were in the possession of the examiner in such a form that corresponding words were easily obtained for use in this test.

In the administration of a test the examiner selects the fourth, fifth, and sixth words which the pupil had wrong on Test 1 (the seventh to tenth words having already been used in Test VII) and matches them from the given lists with two groups of three words each of approximately equal difficulty. Thus nine words are studied in this test. For purposes of the experiment, the order in

[2] The lists are given in Appendix B.

which the words were studied was rotated, i.e., the words of the first list were studied visually by the first pupil tested, kinaesthetically by the second pupil, and auditorily by the third, and correspondingly for the other two lists. In this way the effect of differences in the difficulty of words in the different lists and the effect of order on the three methods of study were largely rotated out.

The visual method of studying a word consists chiefly in looking at the word, looking for hard spots, writing it, and comparing the written product with the original (typed on a card) by carefully looking at both. The auditory method of studying a word consists in using the word in a sentence and spelling it orally as often as desired. The kinaesthetic method consists in writing the word but not looking at the written product. The pupil's writing hand and paper are covered with a manila folder while he tries to get the "feel" of a word. The complete instructions for this and the other tests in the diagnostic battery are given in Appendix B.

The usual time for administering Test III, the Diagnostic Battery, was from forty-five to fifty-five minutes. The tests were given by the writer and four selected examiners who had wide individual testing experience and who were trained by the writer in the administration of the battery. The scoring and interpretation of all tests was checked by at least two of the examiners. Directions for administering and scoring are given in Appendix B.

IV. *Auditory Acuity*

The Bell Laboratories 2-A Audiometer was used to determine the auditory acuity of the subjects of the normal and retarded groups. A description of the instrument may be found in Phillips and Rowell's book on hearing. [54] The tests were administered by a trained examiner in a room where extraneous noises were reduced as much as possible.

In taking the test the subject was seated a few feet from the examiner with his back to the examiner and the instrument. An ear-phone was then applied to the ear being tested. The other ear was left uncovered during the examination.

The 2-A Audiometer allows the intensity or volume of sound heard in the ear-phone to be raised or lowered for each of the pitches created by 64, 128, 256, 512, 1024, 2048, 4096, and 8192 vibrations per second. The intensity for each frequency was raised until the subject indicated with his hand that the sound was heard. This point was recorded in terms of decibels, which is the standard unit for measuring auditory acuity. The volume was then lowered until the subject indicated he could no longer hear the vibration. This point was also recorded in decibels. The midpoint between the two readings was then taken as the index of hearing acuity for the particular frequency. Both ears were tested by this technique for each of the eight frequencies, and percentage hearing losses were derived for them on the total range and on the speech range (512, 1024, and 2048 vibrations).

V. *The Betts Visual Sensation and Perception Series*

The Betts Visual Sensation and Perception Series comprises a number of tests designed to measure visual factors which may be associated with poor reading. It is fully described in Betts' book on reading, *The Prevention and Correction of Reading Difficulties.* [4 : 323 - 50] By use of the Keystone Ophthalmic Telebinocular,[3] the Series is designed to measure binocular vision, far-point fusion, visual acuity, vertical imbalance, stereopsis level, lateral imbalance, near-point fusion, and ametropia. Three experienced examiners gave the tests individually. Children who wore glasses were tested with and without them.

The reliability of the Telebinocular Series has not been fully established by Betts or others. Gates and Bond found that for twenty-six "dull-normal" pupils just beginning school "eighty-one per cent of the pupils show test results which suggest the advisability of a more careful visual examination" on one or more of the tests, but add that "In comparison with data obtained on some of the older children this is a surprisingly large proportion." [30 : 35] They also state, "It might be expected that the variability of performance, whether due to physical conditions, level of attention,

[3] Keystone View Company, Meadville, Pennsylvania.

influence of distractions, different interpretation of directions, and the like, would be greater among these young children in the dull-normal range just entering school than among older, more experienced and brighter pupils." [30 : 32]

VI. *Speech Schedule and Recording*

The speech measure used was the Sherman Articulation Test [4] (Third Grade Form), which is designed as a test of accuracy of pronunciation and articulation. The test is composed of twenty sentences which include most of the common sources of error in articulation. The sounds are so arranged in various words of the sentences that they must be spoken initially, medially, and finally. For example, sentence one, "He saw the best horses" requires the "s" sound to be given in these ways in the words "saw," "best," and "horses" respectively. In addition to the Sherman Test the subjects read four selections of poetry of different meters.

The reading of the sentences of the Sherman Test and the poetry selections was recorded by means of the Electrograph produced by Mr. Walter C. Garwick of Rye, New York. The recordings allowed for approximately seven minutes of speech; in cases where the subject read the sentences and poetry in less time he was encouraged to talk freely on any subject he chose. The recording of the speech in the specially designed sentences, the poetry, and in some cases ordinary conversation, made possible a speech record which could be studied carefully.

The records of the matched pairs were analyzed and checked by a graduate student of the department of speech of Teachers College, Columbia University. On a specially prepared form the wrong articulations in the key words, other mispronunciations, and additions, insertions, omissions, substitutions, and transpositions were recorded. The reading of the poetry was rated for rhythm on a scale of 1 to 5. The reading was rated not only for rhythm in the sense of meter but in terms of "rhythmic patterns" which involve grouping or phrasing, emphasis, movement, and an

---

[4] Used by written permission of the author, Irene Sherman, Winona Public Schools, Winona, Minnesota.

apparent appreciation of the thought of the whole passage. The use of these different, unstandardized tests was necessitated because, to the knowledge of the writer, no adequate standardized speech test measuring articulation, pronunciation, rhythm, etc., is available.

The results of the analysis were checked by two other persons who are recognized as competent judges in the field. The results, which are given in Chapter V, indicate the need of more judges or a more reliable test, or both, than were available in this experiment.

VII. *Gates Silent Reading Tests* (*Grades 3 to 8*)

Types A and D of these well known tests were administered to the matched pairs. Type A, Reading to Appreciate General Significance, involves reading for the main thought of a series of paragraphs rather than for the specific ideas in them. Type D, Reading to Note Details, involves the latter function for a series of short paragraphs. [26] The norms for these tests are based on three hundred thousand cases. The tests were all given by the same examiner, thereby assuring approximate uniformity of administration.

Including the intelligence test and original Modern School Achievement Test, then, a total of eighteen test results are available in comparing the matched pairs of the normal, or better, and the retarded spellers. All the tests were given individually with the exception of the Modern School Achievement Spelling Test, the group intelligence tests for certain of the pairs, and the handwriting tests. The results of the eighteen tests are analyzed by groups in the following chapters.

CASE STUDY

The case study described below properly belongs with the results of the investigation; it is included under procedure as it illustrates rather completely the data which were gathered, not only for this particular matched pair, but for each of the pairs used in the study. It also illustrates that a syndrome may be associated with spelling disability and thus tends to be typical of a considerable number of cases in the study.

Identifying Data

J.K., Girl, I.Q. 106 (S.B.), terms 7, C.A. 9-7, Sp. Gr. 4.5, P.S. 43.
M.R., Girl, I. Q. 108 (S.B.), terms 7, C.A. 9-1, Sp. Gr. 2.5, P.S. 43.

The difference in the *spelling ability* of the two girls is about two years. On the Modern School Achievement Test J had 30 words correct of 55 attempted and M had 4 correct of 54 attempted. In the first twenty words wrong J had 2 additions, 2 insertions, 16 omissions, 12 substitutions, 1 transposition, and no phonetic spellings; M had 4 additions, 6 insertions, 8 omissions, 10 substitutions, 1 transposition, and 3 phonetic errors. While J's types of errors followed more or less the regular pattern for her group, M's errors showed a much higher percentage of additions, insertions, and phonetic spellings than did the complete groups. In the oral spelling test (Diagnostic Battery Test I) neither one had a consistent method. J again had a high percentage of omissions and substitutions (the usual thing in the groups as a whole), while M again showed a comparatively large number of additions and insertions. In the other spelling test (Diagnostic Battery Test 9) out of three words each, J had 2, 2, and 1 correct by the visual, auditory, and kinaesthetic methods respectively; M had 2, 0, and 0 correct in the same order. These differences in spelling ability may be accounted for by some of the following comparisons of the subjects.

J's parents speak Russian and Spanish to one another and English to the child. M's parents speak Spanish to one another and English to the child. M is learning Spanish.

Some differences in *academic achievements* were shown on the pronunciation test. J's grade score was 4.7, M's only 2.9. J used syllables in working out new words and her blending was rated good; M guessed the word as a whole and her blending ability was rated poor.

On the other reading tests, the Gates Silent Reading Type A, J had 13 out of 14 paragraphs correct while M had 3 out of 6 paragraphs correct, with grade scores of 6.1 and 3.1 respectively. On Type D, J had 29 out of 29 correct; M had 6 out of 10 correct, with grade scores of 5.4 and 3.3 respectively. J is undoubtedly the more rapid and accurate reader.

The speech scores indicated that J recorded more errors than M. She had a noticeable foreign accent. She read "toot" for "tooth," "fiolets" for "violets," "cabbatches" for "cabbages," etc., on the Sherman Articulation Test. She made 7 errors in the key words of the Sherman test and 20 other mispronunciations. In reading the poetry she said "de" for "the," "dat" for "that," "worl" for "world," etc. M's only error on the Sherman key words was "wite" for "white." She made 11 other mispronunciations, omitting final "t" sounds, saying "wit" for "with," and like J, "de" for "the." On the rhythm score, however, J was rated 4 and M was rated 3. While the data are incomplete, they indicate that the speech errors do not particularly affect the type of spelling errors in either case.

One of the largest differences in grade score was in the spelling of nonsense words of two syllables, Test 5 of the Diagnostic Battery, in which J's score was 4.1 and M's was 1.95. M spelled "algoat" for "argos," "pikictl" for "piptuk," etc. J spelled by digraphs and by syllables; M spelled letter by letter and by digraphs. The former was rated fairly consistent in method, the latter not.

Other academic achievements showed few differences. The quality of handwriting was the same for both, 7.6, and speed in letters per minute was 48 and 42 for J and M respectively.

In *methods of study,* J used only three different techniques; she pronounced the word, wrote the word looking at the original, and then wrote the word not looking at the original, some seven times, a total of approximately eleven different efforts.[5] M also used three different techniques. Her eyes moved over the word several times; she wrote once looking at the word, and she spelled orally letter by letter twice, a total of approximately four different efforts per word. J's method was described as "Method of attack deliberate, thorough concentration, procedure the same for all." M's method

[5] For explanation of "techniques" and "efforts" see page 69.

was described as "Method of study erratic; did not concentrate on the task and was very restless."

In the visual, auditory, and kinaesthetic test both girls were described as reacting best to the visual method. J tended to make omissions such as "mesure" for "measure" and substitutions such as "estamate" for "estimate." M's errors were more extreme; she wrote "trl" for "travel," "feac" for "factory," "avesent" for "advance," etc.

In the area of possible *constitutional difficulties,* both girls were of normal intelligence, I.Q.'s 106 and 108 (Stanford Binet). Both passed all the fifteen sub-tests of the Betts Series except that J showed some astigmatism in the left eye. On the reversals test J had one reversal and one other error; M had no reversals but 14 other errors.

In the auditory discrimination test J had all correct and M confused "dim" and "din." On the audiometer results a much greater difference was evident. On the total range J had an average per cent loss of -1 and -2 for the right and left ears, while M had an average per cent loss of 12 and 15 respectively. In the speech range J's best ear loss was -4 per cent and M's best ear loss was 13 per cent, a difference of 17 per cent in auditory acuity.

The examiner rated the *attitude* of the subjects to the diagnostic battery and spelling generally as J good and M poor. J liked the tests and "likes spelling very much." M was restless, shy, and "responses had to be dragged out."

Summary of Case Study. Including the somewhat subjective ratings of attitude, certain specific factors appear to be associated with the two years' difference in spelling ability of J and M. J's word recognition and method of working out new words (syllabication and blending) and her speed and accuracy of reading for comprehension are all superior to M's. J is superior in giving letters for letter sounds, spelling nonsense syllables, and particularly in spelling nonsense words of two syllables. In other words, J shows more of a foundation on which to build correct spelling responses.

The methods of studying new hard words differ in that J uses more "efforts" for any one word and uses a suitable check on achievement by writing the word, not looking at the original, and afterward comparing her product and the original. M uses only four "efforts" for each word with no check on her learning.

An important factor is that of 17 per cent difference in hearing loss in the ordinary voice range. M's handicap in this is shown in her relatively high proportion of addition and insertion errors and her writing of words which do not resemble the original word.

The differences in spelling ability, then, may be attributed in part to differences in knowledge and use of word elements and words, effort in word study, a constitutional difference in hearing acuity, and possibly in attitude toward spelling.

Summary

The Modern School Achievement Test in spelling was given to 1185 pupils of grades 3, 4, and 5 in four New York City public schools. On the basis of available records sixty-nine pairs of children were matched individually as to school, sex, grade, chronological age, I.Q., and terms (half-years) in school. One of each pair was normal or better in spelling; the other was one year or more retarded. The differences in spelling grades for the 69 pairs ranged from one to three years, with a mean difference of slightly over two years.

In addition to the intelligence test and spelling test, each pupil was given sixteen different tests of constitutional and academic status. The tests included tests of handwriting, a battery of nine diagnostic spelling and reading tests, tests of vision, hearing, speech and silent reading, all but three of which were given individually. The various tests are described in Chapter III.

A case study illustrates the variety of test results obtained for each of the sixty-nine matched pairs used in the study and that a syndrome may be associated with spelling disability.

CHAPTER IV

SPELLING DISABILITY AND RELATED CONSTITUTIONAL FACTORS

THIS CHAPTER deals with intelligence, vision, audition, and kinaesthesis in relation to spelling disability. Since temperament and attitude are probably more closely related to constitutional factors than to academic achievements or methods of study, observations of them in the two groups are also included. Such constitutional factors as nervousness and emotional stress, various types of glandular imbalance, poorly co-ordinated attention, and poor health and stamina need more investigation than was given in this study concerning their relation to disability in spelling and the other school subjects.

INTELLIGENCE

Gates has said, "Excepting children with I.Q.'s below 70, or those very seriously affected with obvious physical handicaps, I have never yet seen a case, however hopeless he might superficially appear to be, who did not learn to read reasonably well when diagnosed and given remedial instruction by a well trained person." [29 : 111] If reading is possible for children of 70 I.Q. it would seem that the spelling of easy words is possible at the same level, since it may not involve comprehension of so large a number of related ideas as is necessary in reading.

In the present study the lower limit of I.Q. was fixed at 80. The range of I.Q. is from 81 to 132 and the means of the normal and retarded groups are 102.65 and 101.52 respectively (Table 2). The zero order correlations between mental age and spelling grade were obtained separately for the normal and the retarded groups. In the normal group $r = .69$; in the retarded group $r = .67$. But since these groups were also matched on terms in school it becomes necessary to eliminate the effect of the terms. Between mental age and spelling grade, with the effect of terms in school partialled out, $r = .39$[1] for the normal group and $r = .27$[1] for the retarded group.

VISION

Chapter I states that the importance of visual perception is accepted in the present investigation and accordingly is studied here only incidentally. The tests used in the study were the Betts Keystone Telebinocular Series and the Gates Reversals Test.

The Betts series is composed of fifteen sub-tests which are named and defined [3 : 42, 3] as follows:

1, 2.   Far and Near Point Fusion—the mental blending of the right and left eye images into one composite image.

3, 4.   Lateral Imbalance, Far and Near—a tendency for one or both eyes to deviate inward or outward from their normal position.

5.   Vertical Imbalance—a tendency for one eye to deviate upward or downward.

6.   Stereopsis—depth perception.

7-12.   Ametropia—an error of refraction, such as far-sightedness, myopia, or astigmatism.

13-15.   Visual acuity—both eyes, left eye and right eye.

The above results as to passed, failed, or doubtful were obtained by applying the instructions of the Betts Manual to the numerical scores obtained. The second half of Table 3 comparing the two groups indicates that the percentage passing the tests is higher in the retarded spelling group for all tests except that of far-point fusion. The differences for the most part are less than ten per cent of the sixty-one cases and the critical ratios indicate that they are far from reliable.[2] The differences in favor of the retarded

---

[1] Letting 1 represent spelling grade, 2 mental age and 3 terms in school, the formula used was:

$$r_{12 \cdot 3} = \frac{r_{12} - r_{13}\, r_{23}}{\sqrt{1 - r^2_{13}}\, \sqrt{1 - r^2_{23}}}$$

[2] In Chapters IV to VII of this study the word "reliable" when applied to differences is used in its statistical sense. The statistical treatment ascertains the critical ratio, which is the ratio of each difference to its standard error. From this ratio

group may be noted on the near-point fusion and near-point lateral imbalance (C.R.'s of -1.5 and -2.5 respectively). On these tests we find a higher percentage of failures among the normal spellers than among the retarded spellers.

Such differences in eye structure which apparently favor slightly the defective eye are interesting in light of a report by Farris on the effect of visual defects on the reading progress of 1685 seventh grade pupils. He states that "261 pupils affected with hyperopic astigmatism, myopia, myopic astigmatism, ocular muscle imbalance and miscellaneous eye defects of high degree made somewhat greater progress in reading than did an equal number having emmetropic (the so-called normal) eyes." [17 : 96] As Farris points out, this should not be interpreted to mean that visual defects are an advantage in reading, but there may be some doubt that the so-called normal eye, efficient at a longer distance than reading distance, is necessarily most efficient in the reading or study of words for spelling purposes. Farris suggests that myopic pupils make greater progress "because myopic eyes adjust themselves to reading with less exertion of the muscles of accommodation and less expenditure of nerve energy, due to the fact (contrary to popular opinion) that the myopic eye is physiologically superior in structure to the emmetropic eye." [17 : 97] Another possibility is that children with visual disabilities are less competent in games and sports and so tend to improve their reading (and spelling) by more practice. Differences obtained in this study on most of the Betts Tests are so slight that no definite trend can be implied.

The vision of the normal and retarded groups was tested fur-

---

there can be determined the probability that from a population in which the difference was actually zero, a random sample would show a difference as large as the observed difference or larger, due solely to the accidents of sampling and not to the presence of such a difference in the population itself. A critical ratio of 3 indicates a difference of such a size with respect to its standard error as would be produced by accidents of sampling less than one in one hundred times. Therefore, it seems reasonable to assume that a critical ratio of 3 or more indicates a difference which has not been produced by random errors of sampling alone but which exists in the population of which the observed cases are a sampling. If the critical ratio is 3 or more, the differences are here described as "reliable" or statistically "significant."

TABLE 3 Summary of Betts Telebinocular Tests for Normal

| | FUSION | | LATERAL IMBALANCE | | | |
	Far Point	Near Point	Far Point	Near Point	Vertical Imbalance	Stereopsis
Normal Spellers						
No. passed...............	46	31	51	38	61	51
No. failed................	15	26	7	11	0	10
No. doubtful.............	0	4	3	12	0	0
Retarded Spellers						
No. passed...............	42	39	54	50	61	54
No. failed................	15	18	7	7	0	7
No. doubtful.............	4	4	0	4	0	0
Per cent passes—normal......	75.4	50.8	83.6	62.3	100	83.6
Per cent passes—retarded....	68.8	63.9	88.5	82.0	100	88.5
Difference ($P_N - P_R$)	.066	−.131	−.049	−.197		−.049
S.E. difference*.............	.081	.088	.062	.079		.063
C. R......................	.81	−1.5	−.79	−2.5		−.78

* Standard Errors of the Difference for this and other tables involving differences of percentages
Errors and Probable Errors of Percentages for Varying Numbers of Cases," *Journal of Applied*

ther by the Gates Reversals Test (Diagnostic Series VIII 1). Of the 69 subjects in the normal group 4 made a total of 5 reversals. In the retarded group 25 subjects made a total of 52 reversals. A score of 3 or 4 reversals indicates the need of further study for a reading difficulty; as one reversal usually means a spelling error the results have been considered on the basis of any number of errors. The proportion of normal spellers making reversals was .06, retarded .36, giving a difference of 30 per cent and a critical ratio of 4.7. This would indicate that if the difference in the population of matched pairs was zero there is practically no chance that a difference as large numerically as 30 per cent would arise through the operation of random sampling. It would seem probable that more poor spellers make reversals in reading than do good spellers. The causes of such reversals are not a part of this study. The frequency of reversals in the retarded group, however, suggests that a reversals test should be part of a spelling diagnosis.

The fact that no reliable group differences were found on tests of vision does not preclude organic or functional visual difficulties from playing an important role in individual cases of spelling disability. This can best be illustrated by a case study.

and Retarded Spelling Groups (N = 61 for both groups)

| | AMETROPIA | | | | | VISUAL ACUITY | | |
| 3.00 | | 0.50 | | 0.00 | | Both | Left | Right |
L	R	L	R	L	R	Eyes	Eye	Eye
51	50	36	41	34	31	56	52	56
4	4	14	11	14	13	5	9	5
6	7	11	9	13	17	0	0	0
51	51	37	42	34	31	59	55	57
1	5	12	11	14	12	2	6	4
9	5	12	8	13	18	0	0	0
83.6	82	59	67.2	55.7	50.8	91.8	85.2	91.8
83.6	83.6	60.7	68.8	55.7	50.8	96.7	90.2	93.4
	−.016	−.017	−.016			−.049	−.05	−.016
	.068	.089	.084			.041	.059	.048
	−.24	−.20	−.19			−1.2	−.85	−.33

were obtained through use of tables in Edgerton, H. A. and Paterson, D. G., "Tables of Standard *Psychology*, 10, 1926, pp. 378–391.

CASE STUDY

A case study illustrating visual difficulties follows. The results are summarized for the matched pair to illustrate visual differences (for a more complete pair case study, see Chapter III).

W.V., Boy, I.Q. 125 (Pintner-Cunningham), Terms in school 5, C.A. 8-5, Spelling Grade 3.8, P.S. 165.

G.B., Boy, I.Q. 119 (Pintner-Cunningham), Terms in school 6, C.A. 8-2, Spelling Grade 2.2, P.S. 165.

The spelling grades of the boys differ by over one and one-half years. In the first twenty errors on the Modern School Achievement Spelling Test, W had 1 addition, 2 insertions, 13 omissions, 5 substitutions, 2 transpositions, and 2 phonetic errors. For the same G had 3 additions, 4 insertions, 17 omissions, 12 substitutions, 1 transposition, and 1 phonetic error. Several other errors approximated phonetic errors and after the first twenty errors G wrote such words as "klam" for "claim," "dosn" for "dozen," etc.

W revealed no specific defects. His oral spelling was even better than his written and his pronunciation grade higher still, 4.8 and 5.1 respectively. In studying new words he used only two techniques, saying the word once and spelling it orally about eight

times while looking at the original word. His only consistent difficulty on Tests 7 and 9 of the Diagnostic Battery was with double
consonants. He had all words correct on the auditory discrimination test. In Test 9 of the battery (using the visual, auditory, and
kinaesthetic methods) he had the following correct, visual 2, auditory 3, kinaesthetic 1. He said that he liked the visual method best
and he needed considerable time on the auditory method. His silent reading grades were especially high for his grade, 7.1 and 5.9.

W's scores on the vision tests are of particular importance. He
made no reversals and had no other errors on the Gates Reversals
Test. On the Betts Telebinocular Series he failed on 3 of the 15
sub-tests, the ametropia tests for both eyes at an infinite distance
and for the right eye at 80 inches.

In comparison, G's scores are relatively lower on most tests. His
oral spelling and pronunciation grade scores of 2.4 and 2.8 and his
silent reading grades of 2.8 on both types approximate his spelling
grade. His score for giving letter for letter sounds (Diagnostic
Battery, Test 3) is relatively high, grade score 5.5, and is in keep-
ing with his phonetic spelling mentioned above. He uses an average of 4 techniques and 13 efforts in studying a word, but the comment is that his attention wanders. In Test 9 of the Battery (using
the visual, auditory, and kinaesthetic methods) he had the following correct, visual 0, auditory 1, and kinaesthetic 1. His initial
sounds are correct in all words and again there is a predominance
of phonetic errors. He writes "mtay" for "empty," "enuf" for
"enough," "sents" for "since," and "belt" for "built."

In view of this dependence upon the sounds of words the vision
tests are of interest. On the Gates Reversal Test G had 5 reversals
and 17 other errors. On the Betts Telebinocular Series he failed on
six of the fifteen sub-tests and was scored doubtful on three others.
He failed on the far-and near-point fusion tests, the ametropia
tests for both eyes at 80 inches and an infinite distance, and was
doubtful on the lateral imbalance near-point and the other
ametropia tests.

Summary of Case Study. The difference in spelling ability of
the two boys may be traced largely to visual factors. The retarded

speller's scores on the Reversals and Telebinocular tests, and his appeal to the sound of words rather than their appearance, in writing them, indicate definite difficulties in visual perception.

AUDITION

The hearing losses on the 2-A Audiometer were treated separately for the total range and the speech range of the audiometer vibrations. In the normal group only 4 subjects, and in the retarded group only 3 subjects, had a per cent loss greater than 10 per cent for the best ear on the total audiometer range. On this range 45 of the normal group and 50 of the retarded spelling group had hearing losses for the best ear of 5 per cent or less. Table 4 gives the results for the groups.

TABLE 4

Audiometer Per Cent Hearing Losses of Best Ear for Normal and Retarded Spellers
(62 each group)

	Normal Mean$_x$	S.D.$_x$	Retarded Mean$_y$	S.D.$_y$	$\dfrac{D}{M_x - M_y}$	r_{xy}	σ_D	C.R.$_\sigma$
1. Total range......	2.89	3.76	2.21	3.92	.68	.32	.57	1.19
2. Speech range.....	1.95	3.41	1.50	3.14	.45	.19	.53	.85

The difference between the means of the groups is less than one per cent and may be due to random sampling. This supports the statement that constitutional factors such as hearing are seldom factors in a total group situation, but this fact does not preclude them from being of considerable influence in an individual case. (See case study following.)

The difference, if any, favors the retarded spelling group. Gates and Chase have shown that hearing loss may not necessarily affect spelling ability. [31]

In an effort to find whether a hearing difficulty affected the types of errors made (additions, insertions, etc.) subjects were selected who on the total audiometer range were likely to have auditory difficulties. The 13 subjects selected, 9 from the retarded and 4 from the normal spelling group, had a 10 per cent loss in each ear or a high loss in one ear. The types of errors made by the hearing disability group were compared with the errors made by their matched pairs and the total normal spelling group. The results are summarized by percentage as follows:

Type of Error	Hearing Disability Group (N = 13)	Matched Members of Pairs (N = 13)	Normal Spellers (N = 69)
Additions...................	5.3	3.1	3.7
Insertions..................	10.8	8.4	9.5
Omissions..................	38.8	37.1	41.6
Substitutions..............	36.8	37.4	33.4
Transpositions.............	4.3	8.4	5.3
Phonetic Errors............	3.9	5.6	6.2

These results indicate that there are no important differences educationally in the types of errors made by the group with the auditory difficulties, as analyzed above. The statistical analysis of the results also indicates no reliable trends.

The data on auditory discrimination reveal a greater difference than the above data on auditory acuity. (See Table 5.) The nature of the unstandardized auditory discrimination test used (saying one of 15 pairs of words of similar sound at a distance of six feet) was such that it produced a high proportion of correct responses. Yet there is evidence that the advantage shown by the

TABLE 5

Auditory Discimination of Fifteen Pairs of Similar Words by Normal and Retarded Spellers (Diagnostic Battery Test 8) N = 69

	Normal Mean$_x$	S.D.$_x$	Retarded Mean$_y$	S.D.$_y$	$\dfrac{D}{M_x - M_y}$	r_{xy}	σ_D	C.R.$_\sigma$
No. correct responses (out of 15)........	14.06	1.68	12.86	1.62	1.20	−.095	.28	4.3

normal spelling group is not due to errors of sampling. The normal spellers seem to be able to distinguish better such words as "pay" and "bay," "bit" and "big," etc. While the difference of the means is only about 1.2 words in 15, 8 per cent errors in discrimination would affect spelling scores in formal or informal classroom situations.

Case Study

A case study which illustrates the effect of auditory difficulties follows. The case is summarized to illustrate the auditory difficulties (for a case study giving more complete data see Chapter III).

L. B., Boy; I. Q. 102 (S.B.), Terms 7, C. A. 9-7, Spelling Grade 4.8, P. S. 125.

V. M., Boy; I. Q. 102 (S.B.), Terms 7, C. A. 9-2, Spelling Grade 2.8, P. S. 125.

The spelling abilities of the boys differ by about two years. On the Modern School Achievement Spelling Test L had 28 out of 55 correct, V had 7 out of 28 correct (the others were not attempted). In the first twenty errors on the Modern School Achievement Spelling Test, L had no additions, 1 insertion, 11 omissions, 14 substitutions, 1 transposition, and 3 phonetic spellings. V had no additions, 5 insertions, 8 omissions, 13 substitutions, 2 transpositions, and no phonetic spellings. From the first easy words V's spelling is characterized by rather extreme errors such as "deray" for "dried," entire omission of "lame," etc.

L's test results show a relatively regular and satisfactory achievement in the various tests. His parents speak Jewish and English. He impressed the examiner as a capable, rather stolid boy. His reading speech was slow with only 7 and 6 paragraphs attempted on Types A and D respectively. His other weakness seemed to be in Tests 3, 4, and 5 on the Diagnostic Battery, the giving of letters for letter sounds and spelling of nonsense syllables and words. His methods of learning new words included a careful check on the appearance of the word.

In view of V's results below, it should be noted that L's score on the auditory discrimination was 15 (perfect) and that on Test 9 his score for words studied visually was 2, auditorily 3, and kinaesthetically 1.

V is a small, thin boy, somewhat nervous in manner; he has English-speaking parents. His oral spelling and pronunciation tests approximated his Modern School Achievement spelling grade. On Test 3 of the Diagnostic Battery, giving letters for letter sounds, his grade score was 1.8, and on both Tests 4 and 5, spelling one nonsense syllable and nonsense words of two syllables, he had none correct. He gave "pue" for "ub," "sit" for "sot," "mek" for "mip," "sofrar" for "sopot," etc. Unlike L, he did not syllabicate on Test 5.

This apparent auditory difficulty was confirmed in Tests 8 and 9. In the auditory discrimination test his score was 9 out of 15 and the second lowest for all the retarded group. On Test 9 his score on words studied visually was 2, auditorily 0, and kinaesthetically 1. His ordinary method of studying words was simply to write each word fifteen times without stopping to use visual or auditory clues.

A further auditory difficulty was evidenced in the audiometer results. V's per cent hearing losses for the total range were 15 and 22, and for the voice range 11 and 16, for right and left ears respectively. His scores indicate that his hearing may cause school difficulties.

Summary of Case Study. The differences in spelling ability of L and V may be attributed largely to their different methods of studying words and to the latter's disability in auditory discrimination and acuity. V's difficulties in spelling nonsense syllables, handling sound units, etc., seem to be of an auditory nature and are such that they could probably be corrected by stressing visual devices and by individual training directed toward the auditory difficulties here illustrated.

KINAESTHESIS

The relation of kinaesthetic factors to spelling disability has been studied somewhat indirectly in this investigation. Kinaesthetic factors may be involved in speed and quality of handwriting and in rhythm of speech, discussed under academic abilities. Spelling words orally, discussed in the same section, might include rhythm and some kinaesthetic stimuli from movements of lips and throat. The so-called kinaesthetic method (Diagnostic Battery Test 9) involved chiefly movements of the arm and hand.

This test, the only one which attempted directly to explore kinaesthetic factors, was one of three methods of study used in Test 9. It is discussed more fully under methods of study (Chapter VI). The kinaesthetic method was, on the whole, popular with the subjects; this may have been due largely to its novelty. This method showed the least difference between the normal and retarded groups in number of words correct (Table 12). The examiners' comments also showed a trend for the retarded group to do better, comparatively by this method (Table 14). In the normal spelling group comments showed that 6 subjects were stated as being good and 13 subjects were stated as poor on the method. (Poor comments included "became exhausted on kinaesthetic method," "poor with kinaesthetic method," "did not adapt well to kinaesthetic method," etc.). On the contrary, in the retarded spelling group 9 subjects were stated to be "good" in the use of the method and only two subjects were stated to be "poor" in it.

The differences, however, should be interpreted with considerable caution. First, they are too small to have much statistical significance. Second, the poorer spellers may have reacted more favorably to the method because they had a new device in place of old ones which had previously proved unsuccessful. Third, the retarded spellers compare more favorably with the normal group because the latter had fewer words correct by this method than by the other two. In a novel study situation both groups were deprived of their usual means of studying words but the loss meant more to the better spellers who had had good techniques of their own, whereas the poor spellers had less to lose. Fourth, on the so-called auditory method, which involved kinaesthetic factors in the form of lip and throat motor adjustments, the retarded spellers were reliably poorer than the normal group.

With the above cautions in mind, it still seems possible that some poor spellers react better to the system of trying to get the "feel" of words. The retarded spellers had more words correct by this method than by the so-called visual and auditory methods. The role of hand and arm motor movements in spelling is still uncertain. Fernald has promised a discussion of it. [20:5]

TEMPERAMENT AND ATTITUDE

Schonell has emphasized the importance of temperament and personality factors in the spelling success of educated adults. The results of the present study indicate that temperament and attitude may be important also in the spelling success of school children; in the present study it was impossible to explore the field.

All subjects were rated by the examiner on attitude toward the diagnostic battery of spelling tests and toward spelling generally. Each child was asked the question, "What school subjects do you like best?" (and if necessary, "How do you like spelling?") but more stress was laid on the subject's reactions to the diagnostic battery. The somewhat subjective results are summarized in Table 6.

TABLE 6

Attitudes of Normal and Retarded Spellers Toward Spelling and Diagnostic Battery
(N = 69, each group)

Attitude	NORMAL		RETARDED				
	N_x	Per Cent$_x$	N_y	Per Cent$_y$	D	σ_{D}*	C.R.$_\sigma$
Good; likes; excellent; etc.	52	.75	32	.46	.29	.079	3.67
Poor; dislikes; etc.	6	.09	19	.28	−.19	.064	−2.97
Indifferent; fair; bored; etc.	11	.16	18	.26	−.10	.069	−1.45

* From Edgerton, H. A. and Paterson, D. G., *op. cit.*

The table indicates that the "good" and "poor" attitudes seem to apply to good and poor spellers respectively more frequently than would be the case by the effect of random sampling. The rating of "fair" is more doubtful. There is little doubt that favorable attitudes are positively related to school success, but the blending of cause and effect needs further study in spelling and in other subjects.

It was not possible to study general emotional instability, attitudes of inferiority, or apathy toward spelling generally in the present investigation. Certain clues to these may be obtained from the examiners' ratings (Table 6) and their comments on the subjects' methods of study. While certain of the retarded spellers enjoyed the series of tests and certain of the good spellers were bored by them (only one good speller was actually rated "poor" in attitude), a tabulation of the comments reveals that favorable attitudes are characteristic of the good spellers, unfavorable of the poor spellers through all schools and grades involved.

Typical comments on the normal spellers were: "Responded excellently to all three methods"; "Enjoyed visual method best"; "An attractive, quick boy, evidently gifted verbally. He says he likes spelling best; learned such words as 'accommodates' easily." "She says she likes spelling best and spells at home to her mother"; "Said the kinaesthetic method was fun."

Some comments on the attitudes of the retarded group were as follows: "Was sure she couldn't remember words because she was forgetful"; "Method of study erratic, no concentration and very restless; used seven minutes for two words"; "Frequently misspelled words even though he looked at them while spelling"; "Can't grasp more than initial sounds. She is easily discouraged, feels she is stupid and cries easily." Such comments give some insight into attitudes, temperaments, and feelings of inferiority.

The relationships between these and spelling disability need a fuller study than was given them in the present investigation.

The relationship between attitude and achievement, generally, the effect of carelessness on spelling results, the spelling of artistic, original children, and a comparison of the spelling of the docile, willing child with the non-conforming child, are representative topics for further study in the field.

SUMMARY

The chapter deals with the relation of spelling disability to intelligence, vision, hearing, kinaesthesis, and attitude toward spelling.

1. The zero order correlations between spelling grade and mental age for the normal and retarded groups are .69 and .67 respectively. With the effect of terms in school eliminated, on which the two groups were matched, the correlations are .39 and .27 respectively.

2. The Betts Telebinocular Series does not show reliable [3] differences between the normal and retarded groups on any of the fifteen sub-tests. This does not preclude an important effect of defective vision on individual cases; a case study reveals that visual factors may be important in an individual disability.

3. Difference in vision, if any, are in favor of the retarded spelling group. Further study is required to show whether or not pupils with emmetropic (the so-called normal) eyes are more efficient in reading and spelling than children with slight disabilities such as myopia and lateral imbalance.

4. A reliably greater number of retarded spellers make errors on the Gates Reversals Test than do normal spellers. Poor spellers should be examined for reversal tendencies.

5. The tests of hearing acuity on the 2-A audiometer show no educationally significant nor statistically reliable differences in the hearing acuity of the groups of normal and retarded spellers.

6. The types of error (additions, substitutions, etc.) made by 13 of the subjects with greatest hearing loss did not differ significantly from the types of error made by the individuals with whom they were matched or from the types of error made by the whole normal group.

7. On the test of auditory discrimination of pairs of words of similar sound the normal groups made a reliably better score than did the retarded group.

8. Disabilities in auditory acuity and discrimination may affect spelling achievements in individual cases.

9. The role of hand, arm, lip, and throat motor movements in studying spelling requires further investigation.

10. A reliably greater number of normal spellers than retarded spellers were rated "good" in attitude toward spelling and the diagnostic tests.

11. The relationships between attitude and achievement, and between temperamental characteristics and spelling ability require further investigation.

[3] For explanation of "reliable" see page 42.

CHAPTER V

ACADEMIC ACHIEVEMENT AND SPELLING ABILITY

THIS CHAPTER discusses the relation of spelling difficulty to such academic achievements as reading, handwriting, speech, and oral reading, and certain related abilities such as giving letters for letter sounds, spelling of nonsense syllables, and word pronunciation. Blending and syllabication, which are in part academic abilities, are treated in Chapter VI with other methods of word study.

Academic achievement includes the types of errors made in spelling itself. The Modern School Achievement Spelling Tests were analyzed for possible differences between the sixty-nine pairs of the two groups. Out of 3776 words written, the normal spelling group had 1553 or 41.2 per cent wrong. Out of 3574 words written, the retarded group had 2934 or 82.4 per cent wrong. This does not include entire omissions of words, which would bring each total of words written to 3795 words.

This analysis of the errors indicates that omission ("factry" for "factory," etc.) and substitution ("estamate" for "estimate," etc.) are considerably the commonest errors made by each group. Within the limits of the analysis here made, the only types of error in which the groups seem to differ are additions and phonetic errors. There is practically no chance that a difference as large numerically as the one found in additions would arise through random sampling if the general difference between the pairs was zero. The chances are about 2.8 in 100 that a difference as large numerically as the one found in phonetic errors would similarly arise through random sampling. The good spellers tend to make a higher percentage of phonetic errors and the poor spellers are practically certain to make a higher percentage of additions in their spelling errors.

With the exception of the addition of an occasional final "e," additions as measured in this study tend to be rather crude errors

TABLE 7

Types of Errors, by Percentages, of 69 Normal and 69 Retarded Spellers on Modern
School Achievement Spelling Test
(Normal 1693 errors; Retarded 2039 errors)

Types of Errors in First Twenty Words	Normal Per Cent	Retarded Per Cent	D	σ_D*	C.R.σ
1. Additions..............	3.7	6.3	—.026	.0078	—3.3
2. Insertions..............	9.5	9.4	.001	.0099	.10
3. Omissions..............	41.6	38.8	.028	.016	1.8
4. Substitutions..........	33.4	36.2	—.028	.016	—1.8
5. Transpositions..........	5.3	4.3	.01	.0072	1.4
6. Phonetic Errors.........	6.2	4.5	.017	.0078	2.2

* From Edgerton and Paterson, *op. cit.*

showing little appreciation of the appearance or of the sounds of
words ("fielded" for "field," "bloonin" for "balloon," etc.). Phonetic errors, on the other hand, tend to be rather intelligent attempts at the sound of a word whose appearance is unknown. For
example, "wather" for "wait" shows much less appreciation of the
relation between letters and sounds than does "vackashun" for
"vacation" (samples picked at random from the Modern School
Achievement Test). The results of items 4 and 6, Table 7, tend to
show that good spellers have a rather definite knowledge of the
relations between sounds and letters, while retarded spellers have
never acquired this basic knowledge in their first years at school.

In the final test of the correctness of a word, however, it is the
appearance rather than the sound-equivalents which must be
right. Good phonetic spelling can still be consistently wrong in a
language in which the orthography is as peculiar as it is in English.
The evidence is not clear from Table 7 directly that the better
spellers make fewer errors in the general appearances of words.
"Wather" and "wait" look very unlike, whereas "vackashun" and
"vacation" are perhaps less unlike. The normal spellers tend to
make slightly more omissions and transpositions but only the individual errors will show whether or not the appearance of a word
has been changed by these errors. The omission in "stik" for
"stick" does not affect the configuration of the word greatly,
whereas "cas" for "chase" does; in addition to the general appearance, it is necessary, of course, to have the details of appearance

correct for spelling as now used. Since the normal spelling group had twice as many words correct on the Modern School Achievement Test, they were evidently superior in visual perception of the words, both as to general appearances and as to more minute details. The importance of such visual perception was discussed in Chapter II.

READING

The statement that reading and spelling are closely allied is borne out with some clarity in the reading results of the two groups.

The results in Table 8 indicate that the normal spelling group exceeded the retarded spelling group by one year and seven months and one year and three months on Type A, Reading to Appreciate General Significance, and Type D, Reading to Note Details, respectively, of the Gates 3 to 8 Tests. The critical ratios in each item of the above results indicate that, if the population differences were zero in each case, there is practically no chance that differences as large as these would arise through the operation of random sampling. We may be fairly sure, in other words, that a real difference does exist between the normal and retarded spelling groups on each of the six items.

TABLE 8

Reading Grade, Speed, and Accuracy of Silent Reading Measured by Gates 3 to 8
Reading Tests of 61 Normal and 61 Retarded Spellers

| | NORMAL | | RETARDED | | | | | |
	Mean$_x$	S.D.$_x$	Mean$_y$	S.D.$_y$	$\dfrac{D}{M_x - M_y}$	r_{xy}	σ_D	C.R.$_\sigma$
1. Reading Grade, Type A........	5.79	1.61	4.01	1.06	1.78	.379	.20	8.90
2. Reading Grade, Type D........	5.16	1.42	3.85	.64	1.31	.313	.18	7.27
3. No. Paragraphs Attempted, A ..	12.85	3.72	8.48	4.35	4.37	.41	.57	7.67
4. No. Questions Attempted, D..	26.69	6.96	18.46	8.76	8.23	.21	1.29	6.38
5. Per Cent Correct (Accuracy), A..	93.16	9.34	72.05	31.17	21.11	.52	3.55	5.95
6. Per Cent Correct (Accuracy), D..	89.03	10.77	68.69	24.45	20.34	.17	3.22	6.32

The results of columns 3 to 6 of Table 8 indicate that the normal spellers are superior to retarded spellers in both speed and accuracy of reading, whether the reading is for general comprehension or to note details, as defined by the Gates tests. In an effort to analyze such a result further and denoting number attempted by the word "speed," and per cent correct by the word "accuracy," correlations were computed as follows:

1. Speed, Type A, and Spelling Grade, Normal Group, $r = .36$
2. Speed, Type A, and Spelling Grade, Retarded Group, $r = .59$
3. Speed, Type D, and Spelling Grade, Normal Group, $r = .42$
4. Speed, Type D, and Spelling Grade, Retarded Group, $r = .45$
5. Accuracy, Type A, and Spelling Grade, Normal Group, $r = .26$
6. Accuracy, Type A, and Spelling Grade, Retarded Group, $r = .55$
7. Accuracy, Type D, and Spelling Grade, Normal Group, $r = .56$
8. Accuracy, Type D, and Spelling Grade, Retarded Group, $r = .59$

The correlations of both speed and accuracy with spelling grade are considerably smaller on Type A than on Type D in the normal spelling group. That is, for this group neither speed nor accuracy of reading, where the reading is done for general understanding, is so closely related to spelling ability as is speed and accuracy when the reading is done to note details. For the retarded spellers, however, speed and accuracy on Type A are almost as closely related to spelling grade as they are on Type D. That is, within the better spelling group those who read the best for general comprehension may not necessarily spell the best, but within the poorer spelling group the better spellers tend somewhat to be also the better readers for general comprehension. Also when the better spelling group is reading to note details its better readers tend also to be its better spellers. In other words, good spellers may or may not be able to read well for general understanding of a selection but they do seem to possess both speed and accuracy in reading for details. Detailed reading may be positively related to the further analysis needed in word study in spelling.

The correlation coefficients, of course, indicate only slight possibilities, but it seems that ability to read for details, which includes specific word recognition and further word analysis, is more closely related to spelling ability than is reading which gets only the main facts. Some recent investigations in reading show that a pupil can get the general idea of a selection while failing to recognize many of the words in it. If pupils are poor in word recognition they are poor in getting details and may be poor in spelling. It seems possible that poor spelling goes with poor reading for details (rather than a general comprehension) because it goes with crude word recognition.

HANDWRITING

The elements in handwriting have been stated as quality of line, alignment, slant, and shape of letters. The latter would seem to be most closely related to spelling ability in that a badly shaped letter obviously is likely to be marked incorrect. In the present study general quality was studied on the basis of the Thorndike Handwriting Scale in addition to speed in writing.

TABLE 9

Quality and Speed of Handwriting of 68 Normal and 68 Retarded Spellers

Handwriting Characteristics	NORMAL Mean$_x$	S.D.$_x$	RETARDED Mean$_y$	S.D.$_y$	$\dfrac{D}{M_x - M_y}$	r_{xy}	σ_D	C.R.$_\sigma$
1. Quality—Thorndike Scale......	8.64	.88	7.91	.84	.73	.54	.10	7.3
2. Speed—letters per minute........	48.24	17.88	46.00	18.59	2.24	.48	2.26	.99

On the Thorndike Scale the mean score for third grade is 7.8, for fourth grade 8.6, and for fifth grade 9.3. Since at this level a difference of .8 is equivalent to one year, and since the mean difference of the normal and retarded spellers is .73, it may be said that the mean difference for the two groups is almost one year. This is a significant difference educationally, and statistically it has been shown not to be due to the operation of random sampling. The positive relationship may be due to the fact that the better writer, at this level, is the one who writes more—hence must spell more. Another study might investigate the extent to which the shape of letters influences spelling scores or the extent to which handwriting is the function of a carelessness which also extends to spelling.

The score on quality of handwriting in Table 9 was the average of the ratings of five judges. Using split-halves method (correlating judges one plus two with judges three plus four plus five) and applying the Spearman-Brown formula, the reliability of the judgments obtained was $r = .864$.

The difference in speed between the normal and retarded groups of only slightly over two letters per minute would seem to have neither educational nor statistical significance.

SPEECH—ERRORS AND RHYTHM

Within the limitations of the recording apparatus, the reproducing machine, and the sensitivity of the listener to speech deviations, the retarded spelling group made more errors in speech than the normal group except in vowel sounds where the difference was negligible.

Table 10 does not include the record of additions, insertions, and transpositions in speech. The sixty-one normal spellers made a total of 4 additions, 19 insertions, and 2 transpositions; the sixty-one retarded spellers made a total of 12 additions, 23 insertions, and 4 transpositions. The numbers were small for statistical analysis. It may be noted that the commonest types of speech errors, substitutions and omissions, are also the commonest types of spelling errors on the Modern School Achievement Test.

The normal spelling group makes reliably fewer errors in total mispronunciations (outside the key words) on the Sherman Articulation Test and in total errors on all the test (item 7). Total errors include reading errors as well as speech errors, but while certain mistakes are probably reading errors such as "come" for "came," "houses" for "homes," etc., the great majority recorded are pronunciation and enunciation errors such as "lil" for "little" and "dere" for "there." Although the reliable differences indicate a positive relationship between the number of speech and spelling errors, further studies are needed to show what types of speech errors, if any, affect spelling, and how much the relationship may be due to a general language factor.

With the exception of the vowel errors, the differences tend to be

TABLE 10

Recorded Speech Errors and Rhythm of 61 Normal and 61 Retarded Spellers

	NORMAL		RETARDED		$\dfrac{D}{M_x - M_y}$	r_{xy}	σ_D	C.R.$_\sigma$
	Mean$_x$	S.D.$_x$	Mean$_y$	S.D.$_y$				
1. Total Wrong Articulations (Key Words)........	3.48	1.70	4.42	2.46	.94	.18	.352	−2.67
2. Total Other Mispronunciations (Sherman).....	16.30	5.91	20.58	6.72	−4.28	.27	.988	−4.33
3. Total Vowel Errors	2.47	2.07	2.42	1.84	.05	.17	.326	.15
4. Total Consonant Errors.........	6.97	4.35	9.37	7.30	−2.40	.34	.919	−2.72
5. Omissions........	9.52	2.89	10.87	3.51	−1.35	.02	.581	−2.32
6. Substitutions.....	9.40	4.96	12.00	6.48	−2.60	.31	.882	−2.95
7. Total Errors, Additions, Insertions, Omissions, etc. .	19.33	6.25	23.45	7.35	−4.12	.17	1.136	−3.63
8. Rhythm*........	4.11	.77	3.02	.93	1.09	.26	.143	7.62

* For rhythm N = 54 in each group.

reliable on the other items, the chances averaging about .8 in 100 that if the population differences were zero, the differences here found would be due to random sampling and not to a real difference. These items are subdivisions of item 7 in the table.

The subjects were rated for rhythm on a basis of from one to five in reading four selections of poetry. It was pointed out that rhythm is undoubtedly dependent on reading ability but that an attempt was made to measure something more, "rhythmic patterns" depending on phrasing, emphasis, and an apparent appreciation of the thought of the passage. Within the limits of the test and judgments, the normal spellers read with a reliably better rhythm than do the retarded spellers. There is a possibility that some kinaesthetic factor is involved as certain of the poorer readers from the standpoint of errors made a good rhythm score.

Different trained listeners in speech may hear somewhat different errors in speech; the use of one listener is perhaps justified in that he will hear most of the errors of certain types for both the normal and the retarded groups which are being compared.

The differences found between the groups may be expressed, then, in terms of what one listener heard. As a test of reliability of his scoring in this study, the listener repeated his scoring for thirty-five records, selected at random, several weeks after the first scoring was done. The coefficients of reliability for articulation errors (Sherman), for total errors (omissions plus substitutions, insertions etc.), and for rhythm were .80, .79, and .76 respectively.

As a comparison to what a second listener would record, the results of thirty-five records of the first judge were compared to those of a second listener. The coefficient of correlation on item 7, total number of errors made, between the results of the two listeners was only .50, and for rhythm only .45. Applying the Spearman-Brown formula to suggest how closely the averages of these estimates may be made by the same or similar judges on a similar sample of pupils, reliability coefficients were obtained of .67 and .62 respectively. These low coefficients indicate the need for a more reliable method of speech test than was available for this study.

The low reliability of the method used in the present study makes generalizations about the relationships between speech and spelling disability somewhat difficult. Extreme speech defects are rare (Schonell found only four cases in one hundred five pupils) but probably, where they exist, they are very important factors in disability. The relationships between spelling and minor errors of enunciation and pronunciation are not so clear. Within the limits of the method used, reliable differences were found on total errors made, and differences that tended to be reliable on individual types of errors. Correct pronunciation is undoubtedly an aid to the study of a word but this does not necessarily imply that errors in speech cause errors in spelling. Further studies of speech and spelling errors are needed.

CASE STUDY

The following is a case study which illustrates speech and other linguistic difficulties.

G. D., Boy, I. Q. 82 (S.B.), Terms 7, C. A. 10-2, Spelling Grade 2.0, P. S. 43.

G. is a left-handed boy, exceedingly slow in responses; he was co-operative in testing but diffident in attempting anything new. He has a decided foreign accent. He was born in Puerto Rico but came to the United States when he was one year old. His parents speak Spanish to one another and to him.

The following tests were deviates from the usual pattern:

1. On the Gates Silent Reading his grade scores were 2.9 and 3.1. He attempted only two and three paragraphs in Types A and D respectively and his accuracy was 50 per cent and less.

2. He had a perfect score on giving letters for letter sounds but was unable to apply these in combination, with grade scores of 1.6 and below 1.8 in spelling nonsense syllables and words.

3. On the pronunciation test he guessed words as a whole and his blending ability was rated "poor."

4. His study attempts were limited to saying the word once, spelling orally letter by letter three times while looking at the word, and writing it once. He thought the auditory method of study was "too hard" and got none correct on it.

5. His speech record showed the greatest number of errors for any subject in the key words and in other mispronunciations on the Sherman Articulation Test (14 and 36 errors respectively). Some of his errors were "de" for "the," "esk" for "ask," "tretch-ure" for "treasure," "shile" for "child," "fittlers" for "fiddlers," "wa" for "what," etc.

6. Somewhat similar errors were made in his written spelling. He wrote "noke" for "neck," "what" for "wait," "sher" for "chase," etc. Other spelling errors were apparently not closely related to his pronunciation; this may have been due to the limited samplings of both the spelling and the speech records.

7. The per cent hearing loss on the audiometer was 12 and 7 per cent on the total range and 9 and 4 per cent on the voice range for right and left ears respectively. On the auditory discrimination test he failed to distinguish "shall" and "shell," "weather" and "wetter," and "tied" and "tired."

Summary of Case Study. G's mental grade and his language handicaps in foreign background, in reading ability, in disability in combining sounds, in his own foreign accent, and some hearing handicap probably all contribute to his spelling disabilities. While one of these factors may not be enough to cause spelling difficulties, the combination of them probably causes retardation.

OTHER ACADEMIC ACHIEVEMENTS

Other academic achievements which might be related to spelling ability were studied in Tests 2 to 5 of the Diagnostic Battery. Test 1, oral spelling, is also included in this section.

TABLE 11

Various Academic Achievements in Grade Scores of 69 Normal and 69 Retarded Spellers (Diagnostic Battery Tests 1 to 5)

Test	NORMAL		RETARDED		$\dfrac{D}{M_x-M_y}$	r_{xy}	σ_D	C.R.$_\sigma$
	Mean$_x$	S.D.$_x$	Mean$_y$	S.D.$_y$				
1. Oral Spelling.....	4.25	.81	3.01	.67	1.24	.48	.09	13.8
2. Word Pronunciation...........	5.11	.86	3.56	.75	1.55	.61	.07	22.1
3. Giving Letters for Letter Sounds..	3.82	1.49	3.01	.68	.81	−.02	.16	5.1
4. Spelling One Nonsense Syllable ..	4.85	1.85	2.48	1.09	1.37	.10	.25	5.5
5. Spelling Nonsense Words of Two Syllables.......	4.60	1.62	2.38	.88	2.22	.13	.21	10.6

In grade score the retarded group is on the average from eight months to two years two months behind the normal spelling group in these tests of linguistic abilities. In each case the differences are such that, if the population differences were zero, there is practically no chance that differences as large as these numerically could arise through the operation of random sampling.

The mean difference in oral spelling was to be expected as there is ordinarily a high positive correlation between written and oral spelling and the groups were separated on the basis of written spelling. Differences of such high statistical reliability on the other tests indicate considerable relationship between the ability measured in these tests and spelling ability. In particular the test of spelling nonsense words of two syllables (with a mean difference of two years two months) seems to distinguish between the groups. In this test and test 4 the subject is required to use familiar sounds in a novel situation. The results indicate that inability to turn sounds into letters, phonograms, or syllables is probably the basis of much poor spelling. Pupils who have not developed these skills are unable to use techniques fundamental to most spelling, and so are definitely handicapped in spelling attack on new words.

The relationship between retardation in spelling and the above tests suggests that they would form a desirable part of a diagnosis of spelling disability.

Further, the relationships between skilled silent spelling, good silent reading, good oral spelling, good use of word elements singly and in combination indicate the possibility of a *general* linguistic ability as suggested by Traxler [67:35] and others. This would partly explain the existence of handicaps in speech, spelling, written language usage, and reading all in the same individual.

Another explanation arises from the above discussion of academic achievements. Granted a fair measure of ability, academic achievements are based definitely on the instruction and guidance a child receives, particularly in the primary grades. Gates has shown that reading deficiencies may be due to ineffectual types of teaching. He says, "Failure to acquire one or more of the many techniques or skills involved in reading is believed to be a common, if not the most frequent source of the difficulty." [27:12] A considerable number of data accumulated in this chapter indicate that a similar failure to acquire techniques of handling letter sounds, syllables, word analysis, and similarities and differences in sounds and words may be a fundamental cause of spelling disability. Spelling has as its basis certain academic skills which must be effectually learned if disability is not to result.

SUMMARY

The chapter discusses the relation of spelling ability to silent reading, handwriting, speech and oral reading, giving letters for letter sounds, spelling of nonsense syllables, and word pronunciation.

1. The types of errors made on the Modern School Achievement Test were analyzed as to additions, insertions, omissions, substitutions, transpositions, and phonetic errors. The differences in types of errors made by each group did not exceed 3 per cent.

2. The retarded group made a reliably higher percentage of additions in their errors than did the normal group. The normal spelling group tended to make a higher percentage of phonetic errors than did the retarded group.

3. The mean grade score of the normal group was reliably higher than that of the retarded group on the Gates Silent Reading Tests, Grades 3 to 8, Types A and D.

4. The mean speed and mean accuracy of reading scores of the normal group were reliably higher than those of the retarded group.

5. In the normal group there is a suggestion that speed and accuracy of reading for general comprehension is not so closely related to spelling grade as is reading to note details. In the retarded group little difference was found on the different types of reading.

6. The normal spelling groups are reliably better in quality of handwriting as measured by the Thorndike Scale than are the retarded spellers. The difference in speed of writing between the groups is insignificant educationally and statistically.

7. Within the limits of the method used, the retarded spellers made more errors in speech than did the normal spellers except in vowel sounds, where the difference was negligible. The differences are statistically reliable for total mispronunciations and total types of errors and tend to be reliable on other items.

8. The normal spellers are rated reliably higher in "rhythm" than the retarded spellers on the basis of oral reading of poetry.

9. The commonest types of speech errors are the same as the commonest spelling errors on the Modern School Achievement Spelling test—omission and substitution. Further studies are needed to investigate the relationships between speech and spelling errors.

10. The reliability of the results obtained by comparing the records of errors obtained by two different listeners suggests the need of an improved test of speech.

11. A case study illustrates that a speech handicap, combined with certain related factors, may be a cause of spelling disability.

12. The normal spelling group had reliably higher scores than did the retarded group on each of the following tests: oral spelling, word pronunciation, giving letters for letter sounds, spelling nonsense words of one and two syllables.

13. Inability to turn sounds into letters, phonograms, or syllables is probably a basic cause of poor spelling.

14. The rather striking agreement between these tests and others involving language usage suggests the possibility of a general linguistic ability, evidenced by facility in handling words well in various ways.

15. The data of the chapter indicate that spelling disability is often caused by failure to acquire in the primary grades techniques of handling letter sounds, syllables, word analysis, similarities and differences in words, and other basic language skills. Within certain limits of ability, the failure is pedagogical.

CHAPTER VI

METHODS OF STUDY AND SPELLING DISABILITY

GROUP DIFFERENCES

THE DIFFERENCES found between the normal and retarded spelling groups in method of attack or learning new words throw considerable light on factors associated with spelling disability. In Test 7 of the Diagnostic Battery the subject was asked to learn to study four words, incorrectly spelled on Test I of the battery, in the way he usually studied hard words. He was timed on each word. In addition, space was left for comments on method of work for each word and the examiner used a check list of fifteen items indicating his method of study. These were:

Pronounces correctly; eyes move over word several times; closes eyes to recall appearance; looks at word, saying clearly; fixes on hard part; eyes closed a second time; writes looking at word; writes without looking at word; writes word twice or more; spells orally letter by letter looking at word; spells orally letter by letter without looking at word; spells by syllables looking at word; spells by syllables without looking at word; spells orally by units without looking at word; and spells orally by units looking at word.

From this check list and the accompanying comments a great many data were collected on how these children study words when asked to do it "as you usually do."

The first fact that appears from Table 12 is that the normal and retarded spellers do not differ significantly in the time spent studying words as they usually study them. The second fact that appears is that many children use relatively few different techniques in studying words. It is common to find children in both groups using only two or three of the above list of fifteen items recommended by writers who stress the need of various avenues of approach.

TABLE 12

Methods of Studying Hard Words in Tests 7 and 9 of Diagnostic Battery
for 69 Normal and 69 Retarded Pupils

Methods	NORMAL Mean$_x$	S.D.$_x$	RETARDED Mean$_y$	S.D.$_y$	M_x-M_y	r_{xy}	σ_D	C.R.$_\sigma$
Test 7								
Times in seconds studying 4 words..	327.93	178.11	314.28	186.36	13.65	−.0034	31.2	0.44
No. correct.......	2.16	1.28	1.39	1.21	.77	.36	.17	4.5
No. techniques used per word.......	3.68	1.21	3.68	1.01	0.0	−.11	.20	0.0
No. efforts used per word............	10.15	5.39	10.12	5.94	.03	.08	.93	0.03
Test 9								
No. Visual correct.	1.74	.94	1.39	.97	.35	−.07	.17	2.1
No. Auditory correct..............	1.77	.98	1.28	1.01	.76	.12	.16	4.8
Kinaesthetic correct..............	1.61	.85	1.46	.98	.15	.20	.14	1.1

The third fact shown by the group results is that the normal or better spellers have the same variety of attack as the poor spellers in so far as the fifteen above items are concerned. Both the normal and the retarded groups had identical means of 3.68 different techniques.

Not only did the normal and retarded groups use the same variety of techniques but they repeated them as often. The term "efforts" is here used to apply to the total number of techniques used. For example, a subject that pronounced a word once, closed the eyes to recall the word twice, spelled orally letter by letter three times, and wrote the word without looking at it twice, used a total of four different techniques and eight "efforts" in studying the word. The mean number of efforts used by the normal group was 10.15 and by the retarded group 10.12, with a critical ratio of 0.03. This indicates that not only is the difference insignificant educationally, but it may be due to random sampling.

It should be pointed out that utilizing a larger number of "efforts" may not necessarily be a superior method of studying a hard word. One subject in the retarded group pronounced the word and spelled it orally letter by letter alternately thirty times. With some use of varying techniques a certain amount of repetition is probably desirable, and this amount undoubtedly varies in individual cases. From the above, however, we conclude that the children of the two groups: (1) Tend to use three or four different techniques and about ten different "efforts" in studying a hard word. (2) They use practically the same time and the same number of techniques and "efforts," even though the end results vary considerably. (3) Differences must be due to factors not observed in this rather rough analysis; further analysis is thus necessary.

DIFFERENCES IN INDIVIDUAL TECHNIQUES

Although gross differences were negligible, the analysis of the use of individual techniques in Table 13 reveals considerable differences in the normal and retarded groups. The retarded group on the average pronounces the word reliably oftener than does the normal group. It also uses techniques 10 and 10–1 oftener than the normal group; the difference is not fully reliable for spelling orally letter by letter. The techniques which the retarded use oftener tend to be forms of unthinking attack—saying a word (after the first time) and spelling the word letter by letter require little concentration on the word. On the other hand the normal spellers tend to use more frequently forms of study which may be considered active; they tend to write the word without looking at the original and to spell orally by syllables looking at the word oftener than do the retarded spellers. The first method makes a check on achievement possible; the second is a logical relating of the form of a word to its pronunciation and spelling. The retarded speller tends to use an unthinking attack which utilizes no clues nor other aids to spelling; the normal speller tends to use more active methods, with a check on his achievement.

The results show further that not only do the pupils use far fewer than the nine steps suggested by Horn, but they do not seem to use what would ordinarily be considered the best two or three techniques. Pronouncing a word and spelling orally letter by letter looking at the original word are the commonest techniques in both

Table 13

Use of Fifteen Techniques in Studying a Word in Spelling by 69 Normal and 69 Retarded Spellers—Average of 4 Words

Techniques	NORMAL		RETARDED		D	σ_D #	C.R.σ
	N_x	Per Cent$_x$	N_y	Per Cent$_y$			
1. Pronounces correctly....	131	.19	212	.26	—.07	.022	—3.2
2. Eyes move over word several times............	41	.06	41	.05	.01	.011	.91
3. Eyes closed to recall appearance.............	6	.01	4	.01	o		
4. Looks at word saying clearly..............	15	.02	5	.01	.01	.0064	1.8
5 Fixes on hard part......	4	.01	3	.00	.01		
6. Eyes closed a second time	1	.00	o				
7. Writes looking at word..	66	.09	76	.09	o		
8. Writes word without looking at original........	91	.13	72	.09	.04	.016	2.5
9. Writes word twice or more	25	*.36	18	*.26	.10	.078	1.3
10. Spells orally letter by letter.................	68	.10	111	.14	—.04	.016	—2.5
10–1. Spells orally letter by letter looking at original	118	17	163	.20	—.03	.020	—1.5
11. Spells orally by syllables	48	.07	47	.06	.01	.013	.77
11–1. Spells orally by syllables, looking at original	46	.07	30	.04	.03	.013	2.3
12. Spells by units.........	42	.06	29	.04	.02	.012	1.7
12–1. Spells by units, looking at word..............	24	.03	26	.03	o		
	700	1.01	820	1.02			

* Repetition of No. 8 therefore per cent taken on 69 cases.
# Edgerton, H. A. and Paterson, D. G., *op. cit.*

groups. It was suggested in Chapter III that many pupils may not need to utilize all the visual, auditory, and kinaesthetic techniques which have been suggested. The evidence is fairly clear here that not only do the pupils use only a few techniques but they also tend to use relatively inactive ones. It would seem that one aim of spelling, to provide pupils with techniques for studying new words, has not been realized for all the subjects of this study.

The differences in the methods of the normal and retarded spellers are shown further by the comments made on the systems used.

An analysis of the examiners' comments reveals that a normal speller used fair or good methods of studying words (based on such factors as variety of attack, concentration on the task, consistency, attention to hard parts, checking one's work, etc.) while his matched pair did not. A tabulation of the results indicates that at least 28 of the normal spellers used a definitely "good" method, based on the techniques used and comments of the examiner, while about 9 used a definitely "poor" one. In the retarded group, however, 24 pupils used a "poor" method and only two used a definitely "good" method. Other methods were fair or doubtful.

The following are characteristic comments made by the examiner on the methods used by some of the 28 subjects of the normal group using a "good" method: .

1. "Method of study same for all words; prints as well as writes; spends much time comparing words."
2. "Method of attack is deliberate; thorough concentration."
3. "Method intelligent; insisted on knowing word well when not looking at it."
4. "Wastes time but has a good method of learning by testing himself."
5. "Circles a particular part of a word which he wants to remember."
6. "Learns to spell by finding known small words in given word; remembered words studied this way."
7. "Writing words a few times helped her very much."
8. "In one word he omitted a syllable; discovering this, he relearned the word; did not use writing."
9. "Learned the three words very easily; in fourth word he had to spend much time on 'au' in 'restaurant'."
10. "He is very consistent and concentrates thoroughly on each word."
11. "Tests himself by kinaesthetic and visual methods in more difficult words."
12. "Writes in air and across desk with finger."
13. "Consistent method of study; checking is adequate."

The following are characteristic comments on the methods used by some of the 24 "poor" spellers of the retarded group:

1. "No real method of attack; has difficulty with 'e' and 'a' sounds."
2. "No attempt at system or method; omissions and substitutions were chief errors."
3. "Method of study erratic; no concentration and very restless; used several minutes in studying two words."
4. "Wrote each word ten times."
5. "No real method and no check on learning."
6. "Child was sure she couldn't remember words because she was forgetful."

7. "Inconsistent; learns mainly by studying orally."
8. "Lacked a definite check on learning; in too great a hurry."
9. "Frequently misspelled words even though he looked at them while spelling."
10. "Had the practice of writing a word incorrectly three times or more before checking his performance."

The methods used in studying words were explored further in Test 9 of the Diagnostic Battery which allowed the subjects to study hard words by three methods which were largely visual, auditory, and kinaesthetic respectively. Of the 69 pupils of the normal group, 40 showed a definite preference for one method, while in the retarded group 20 showed a distinct preference for one method to the exclusion of the other two methods. This gives a difference in the percentages in each group of 29 per cent and a critical ratio of 3.6. Accordingly, there is practically no chance that a difference as large as this numerically would arise through the operation of random sampling if the difference between all the matched pairs was zero. The examiners' judgments may be interpreted as meaning that more of the normal group tend to have one well-defined way of going about the study of words, and obviously favor it. It should be noted, however, that nearly one-half the normal group and over two-thirds the retarded group did not show preference for one of the visual, auditory, or kinaesthetic methods to the exclusion of the other two.

A comparison of the particular methods preferred (used best) by those using one method of study shows further differences.

Table 14 indicates that the normal spelling group tends to include more subjects who excel in the visual and auditory methods

TABLE 14

Percentages of Normal and Retarded Spellers Stated by Examiners as Excelling on One Study Method, Test 9, Diagnostic Battery

Method	NORMAL		RETARDED		D	σ_D	C.R. σ
	N_x	Per Cent$_x$	N_y	Per Cent$_y$			
1. Visual..................	19	.28	8	.12	.16	.067	2.4
2. Auditory...............	15	.22	5	.07	.15	.059	2.5
3. Kinaesthetic...........	6	.09	7	.10	−.01	.049	− .20

but approximately the same percentage who excel in the kinaesthetic method. If the numbers of subjects here given as excelling in the kinaesthetic method are compared to the totals for each group who are named as excelling in one (that is, 40 and 20 subjects instead of 69) we find that 35 per cent of the retarded division and only 15 per cent of the normal division favor the kinaesthetic method. This difference is not reliable statistically (a small number of cases are involved) but in the light of the results given below there seems to be a tendency for the retarded spellers to do better on the kinaesthetic method.

A further and more objective analysis of the results of the visual, auditory, and kinaesthetic methods of study is possible in comparing the actual scores made by each group on these tests given in rotated order. Table 12 shows that the normal group utilized the method called auditory reliably better than did the retarded spelling group, and tended to use the visual method more successfully. This should not necessarily be interpreted as meaning that the good spellers are more "auditory minded." It is possible that this method, utilizing as it does only the technique of spelling orally, does not give enough clues to the poor speller previously accustomed to failure. There is some evidence, however, that the good spellers do utilize auditory and visual techniques more successfully than the poor spellers.

The higher relative percentage of retarded spellers preferring the kinaesthetic method has been mentioned above. It is consistent with this evidence that Table 12 shows less difference between the scores of the normal and retarded groups on the kinaesthetic method than it does on the visual and auditory methods. (The difference is only .15 of a word on four words and the critical ratio is 1.1.) The two differences in percentages excelling and in actual scores should not be interpreted as meaning that retarded spellers should be taught by the kinaesthetic method. It may only mean, for example, that the retarded spellers are more used to study methods which involve much writing of words. Writing a word is probably a benefit to many normal as well as many retarded spellers as it may call attention to the parts of a word in their correct sequence. Further, the so-called auditory method of Test 9 was also kinaesthetic in the stricter sense in that it involved motor movements of lips and throat. The possibility of the kinaesthetic method being more useful to the retarded group is suggested but not established by the data of this study. The advantage to the retarded group in the use of these three methods is discussed on page 51.

ORAL SPELLING

An examination of methods used in studying spelling is incomplete without mention of methods observed in oral spelling. Despite the continued popularity of spelling "bees" oral spelling is not considered as useful as written, and methods used in the two are usually not identical. Oral spelling, however, can give definite clues to how a pupil reacts to words and his rhythm in spelling them; it should probably be a part of all diagnostic programs.

Since on Test 1 the normal group were reliably better spellers (C. R. = 13.8), differences in method on the test may be important. The analysis in Table 15 indicates that, whereas only 12 per cent of the normal group used a letter by letter method, 24 per cent of the retarded group used this method, a reliable difference (C. R. = 3.1). Furthermore, the normal group tended to use more spelling by syllables and did more spelling phonetically (i.e., a higher percentage of their errors were phonetic) although not notably so in either case. The phonetic errors follow the silent spelling trend in which the better spellers also made

TABLE 15

Methods of Oral Spelling Used in Diagnostic Battery, Test 1, by 67 Normal and 66 Retarded Spellers (Where not more than 3 methods were used by one subject.)

Method	NORMAL		RETARDED		D		
	N_x	Per Cent$_x$	N_y	Per Cent$_y$	P_N-P_R	σ_D	C.R σ
1. Spells word as a unit.....	26	.20	18	.18	.02	.052	0.38
2. Spells letter by letter.....	12	.09	24	.24	−.15	.049	−3.1
3. Spells by units (digraphs).	45	.36	40	.40	−.04	.064	−0.63
4. Spells by syllables........	30	.23	15	.15	.08	.051	1.6
5. Spells phonetically.......	16	.12	4	.04	.08	.035	2.3
Total.............	129	1.01	101	1.01			

more good guesses from the sound of words, many of which were unfamiliar to them.

The examiners marked the method of spelling orally for consistency by yes, no, fairly. The per cent of yes and no was slightly higher in the retarded group than in the normal group. This is not impossible as in the retarded group there may have been more who used the same method throughout without regard to the form of the word as well as more who had no real method of spelling. In the "fairly consistent" division, however, the normal group had 62 per cent while the retarded had 43 per cent of its subjects (C. R. = 2.3). There is a trend for the better spellers to have some method which they may have varied to suit the form of the various words.

In general, the better spellers tend to utilize an active and somewhat varied oral attack on new words rather than an unthinking repetition such as letter by letter spelling. The good speller is more active in discovering clues in the form of syllables or known smaller words.

One of the normal group (Sp. Gr. 5.8) carried this to what might be considered an extreme. She drew lines around the "elements" in words as she found them. The record of her study of the word "approaches" follows: There is a twin "p," the word "a" and "ch." "Ro" is like row the boat, and it is in the "es" family. "a" in the middle is silent. "App" is like in "apple" and "o" as in orange. There is "aches" in it and the beginning of "April." She wrote the word on the paper provided five times and finally said "I know the word." Another feature of this child's study was the discovery of what she called "sandwiches" such as "iffi" in "difficulty" and "aura" in "restaurant." The above may be analysis taken to absurd lengths but the comments of the examiners on the normal group indicate a rather general active approach to words in such descriptions as "He pronounced words in syllables," "He circles a particular part of a word he wants to remember," etc.

The method of approach to words is undoubtedly influenced by attitude, discussed in a previous chapter, and by training received in the classroom. In view of the importance of the method of attack, devices which attract interest toward words should be a part of any spelling program. This problem is discussed briefly in the following chapter.

Blending and Syllabication

Blending and syllabication are usually a part of study methods as described above; this section gives some additional information about their utilization.

Blending was employed by the subjects of the experiment not only in putting letters together to form syllables and words but in the pronunciation test (Diagnostic Battery Test II). In Test II there was a difference in pronunciation score of over one and one-half years in grade score (C. R. = 22.1) so that the method of attack in pronouncing the words is important. The examiners rated the subject's blending ability as good, fair, or poor.

TABLE 16

Comparison of Normal and Retarded Spellers on Techniques Used in Pronunciation Test (N = 69 in each group)

	NORMAL		RETARDED				
	N_x	Per Cent$_x$	N_y	Per Cent$_y$	D	σ_D	C.R.$_\sigma$
Blending—good............	45	.65	8	.12	.53	.069	7.7
Blending—fair.............	23	.33	20	.29	.04	.079	−.51
Blending—poor............	1	.014	41	.59	.576	.060	9.6
Guesses word as a whole....	11.5	.17	36	.52	−.35	.075	−4.7
Analyzes by syllables.......	49	.72	20	.29	.43	.077	5.6
Analyzes by sound units (digraphs)................	7.5	.11	15	.19	−.08	.060	−1.3

From Table 16 it would appear that blending ability, subject to the limitations of the examiners' judgments, is possessed not only by those excelling in pronunciation but by the group of better spellers. Only one subject in the normal group was rated "poor" in blending in the process of recognizing new words.

There is some evidence that guessing words as a whole is not good technique positively related to spelling ability. Good spellers seem to syllabicate in recognizing new words. (C. R. = 5.6) This evidence is supported in the test of spelling nonsense words of two syllables (Diagnostic Battery, Test 5). Seventy-four per cent of the better spellers used syllabication while only 50 per cent of the retarded spellers used it. The critical ratio indicated a difference not due to sampling errors (C R. = 3.0). Furthermore, the better spellers were reliably more consistent in their method.

Probably the most direct evidence on syllabication was given in the studying of hard words (Diagnostic Battery, Test 7). See items 10–1 and 11–1 in Table 13.

If the difference of the two population groups was zero on the use of oral letter by letter study, the probability that a difference as large as 3 per cent would arise through the operation of random sampling is about 13.3 in 100. If the difference of the two population groups was zero on the use of spelling orally by syllables, the probability that a difference between the groups as large as 3 per cent would arise through the operation of random sampling is about 2.1 in 100. In other words, there seems to be a slight trend for spelling orally letter by letter to be used by poor spellers, while it is fairly certain that spelling orally by syllables is likely to be used by a larger number of the normal group than the retarded group.

The results of Tests 2, 5, and 7 of the Diagnostic Battery indicate that methods such as guessing a word as a whole, spelling it letter by letter for practice, and other such relatively unthinking processes are inferior to such relatively active reactions as seeing parts, blending them, and syllabication.

The case study of a matched pair which follows illustrates that, for a particular case, method of studying words may be a cause of poor spelling.

CASE STUDY

T.D., Girl, I. Q. 95 (S. B.), Terms 6, C. A. 8–11, Spelling Grade 5.3, P. S. 43.

M. L., Girl, I. Q. 100 (S. B.), Terms 7, C. A. 8–11, Spelling Grade 3.3, P. S. 43.

The two girls described show many similarities in test scores with the exception of their written spelling grades above and their methods of studying words. T's parents speak German to each other and to the children; M's parents speak French to each other and to the children. In both homes the children speak English to one another.

On the first twenty incorrect words of the Modern School Achievement Spelling Test, T made one addition, three insertions, eight omissions, five substitutions, two transpositions, and one phonetic error, a not unusual distribution. On the same group, M made two additions, two insertions, eleven omissions, six substitutions, two transpositions, and five phonetic errors. The proportion of phonetic errors is higher than usual.

On *constitutional* factors T failed only on the near-point fusion test in the telebinocular series and M failed only on the ametropia tests for right eye at eighty inches and an infinite distance. On the audiometer results T showed a hearing loss of 8 per cent and 7 per cent for right and left ears on the total range, and of seven and 5 per cent for right and left ears on the speech range. M's hearing was normal in all cases. The girls are both of normal intelligence. T doesn't like spelling "especially" and M likes it.

On *academic achievements* tested (other than written spelling) the girls showed a rather remarkable similarity; where the results were not identical T had an advantage over M of a few months only in grade score. In oral spelling the grade scores for T and M were 3.4 and 3.0 respectively; on pronunciation (Test 2) 4.3 and 2.9 respectively; on Test 3, 2.4 and 2.4; on Test 4, 4.0 and 4.0; on Test 5, 5.6 and 4.9. On the auditory discrimination test each had 14 correct. On Test 9, on the visual, auditory, and kinaesthetic tests, T had 2, 1, and 1 correct; M had 2, 3, and 1 correct. On the Gates tests, T's reading grades were 5.1 and 4.0, and M's were 4.3 and 3.8. The number of speech errors recorded was almost identical in each division.

On *methods of study* these similarities do not exist. On Test 7 T took over five minutes to study the four hard words while M took slightly over a minute and a half. T's method consisted of moving her eyes over the word several times, spelling it orally by syllables not looking at the original, and writing the word. On the whole battery the examiner states that she is "almost completely visual" (her hearing loss was unknown to the examiner at that time.) M's method is to pronounce the word, spell it silently while looking in the air, and to pay attention to what she considers the hard part. She did this very quickly on all words.

On the oral spelling and pronunciation tests the examiner records of T: "She adapts the method to the word—syllabizes for 'travel,' uses digraphs in 'afraid' and spells 'elaborate' phonetically." She attempts the pronunciation of words by syllables and her blending is "good." Of M's oral spelling the examiner records: "She spells very fast and fluently even on unknown words." On the pronunciation test she "tends to turn the words into words she knows on the first trial" but her blending ability is "good."

On the method of study the examiner's final comment for T is: "Method intelligent; insisted on knowing the word well without looking," while M's method is called "rapid and inconsistent."

Summary of Case Study. T has overcome a slight auditory handicap in spelling by developing a careful method of studying words with a check on her achievement. This seems to be largely responsible for her superiority over M who is probably too fast in her study and who lacks a check on her achievement.

SUMMARY

1. When asked to study as they usually do the pupils of both the normal and the retarded groups used an average of only 3.68 different techniques of study. This was from 15 techniques noted by the examiner and is considerably less than the 9 techniques suggested by Horn, Breed and other writers.

2. The normal and retarded groups repeated their techniques approximately the same number of times, i.e., used the same number of "efforts," about ten, per word.

3. The normal and retarded groups differ considerably in the kinds of word study techniques they use. More retarded spellers pronounced the word oftener than the normal spellers and the group tended to spell orally letter by letter more than the normal group. More of the normal spelling group tended to write the

word without looking at the original and to spell by syllables looking at the original than did the retarded group. In general the retarded group used somewhat inactive approaches such as saying the word and spelling by individual letters while the normal spelling group used active approaches such as syllabication and checking their written trials.

4. The pupils of both groups used few techniques, more inactive than active ones, and many showed that they had not mastered a technique of studying new words.

5. The normal spelling group utilized the "auditory" method and tended to use the "visual" method better than the retarded group. On the "kinaesthetic" method the groups showed little difference, with a slight trend in favor of the retarded group.

6. Fifty-eight per cent of the normal spelling group and twenty-nine per cent of the retarded group (a reliable difference) showed definite preference for and capacity in one of the visual, auditory, or kinaesthetic methods to the exclusion of the other two.

7. In oral spelling a reliably higher percentage of the retarded group spelled letter by letter than did the normal spelling group.

8. On the pronunciation test a reliably higher percentage of the normal group were good at blending and analyzed words by syllables than did the retarded group. A reliably higher percentage of the retarded spelling group guessed the words as a whole than did the normal group on the same test. Ability to blend word parts and to syllabicate seems to be positively associated with spelling ability.

CHAPTER VII

SUMMARY AND CONCLUSIONS

For specific statements of the purposes, procedures, and particularly the results of the present study, the reader is referred to the preceding chapter summaries. This final chapter combines the results from various phases of the present investigation, relates them to previous studies, and, from the characteristics of good and poor spellers thus obtained, suggests procedures for spelling programs. Although the results have been combined, some care is taken in the present chapter to distinguish case study findings from more general group results.

This report discusses two or three dozen disabilities or factors associated with disability. The separate discussion of these may tend to imply that they are unitary, independent factors; actually, we find that such is rarely the case with real boys and girls. Even one of the broad divisions of the preceding three chapters, constitutional, academic-achievement, or study-method, does not usually contain all the sources of difficulty for any one of the sixty-nine retarded cases of this investigation. As Traxler says, "While a listing of disabilities and manner of treating them is valuable for purposes of logical analysis, a retarded pupil will ordinarily exhibit, not one disability, but a complex of them, and in varying degrees." [67:18] An analysis of the individual cases in the present study agrees with Gates [28], Schonell [59], Davis [15] and others that a syndrome tends to be connected with spelling disability.

With the above in mind, it is possible to study and discuss some of the specific constitutional, academic-achievement, and study-method factors associated with poor and good spellers.

The *constitutional factor* of intelligence was held constant in the present investigation by matching the poor and good spellers on mental age and chronological age; the one reservation made was that all pupils studied had an intelligence quotient above 80. The coefficients of correlation between mental age and spelling grade, with the influence of terms in school eliminated, were .39 and .27 for the good and the poor spellers respectively. The above result indicates that the poor spelling group, particularly, may contain pupils whose spelling status is not closely related to their mental status; it is not unusual to find one or two bright pupils in a class who are not good spellers. Intelligence does not correlate as highly with spelling grade as does visual perception, where the coefficient of correlation is .55. [20:86] But visual perception includes a group of complex skills and it seems possible that spelling ability is as closely related to intelligence as to any single factor in the constitutional, academic-achievement or study-method areas.

The constitutional factors of visual and auditory acuity are found not to be related to the normal and retarded spelling groups, as groups. If there are any differences in the hearing for different pitches, as measured on the audiometer, and vision, as measured on the fifteen sub-tests of the Betts Telebinocular Series, they give the retarded group slightly better vision and hearing. The results are far from being reliable statistically but probably indicate that slight sensory handicaps do not affect spelling ability. Gates and Chase [31] have shown that the deaf are not particularly handicapped in spelling and Farris found that some visual defects were positively associated with a year's reading gains in a large group of children [17].

Three important exceptions to the above lack of difference should be noted. The retarded spelling group make reliably more errors on the visual test of tendency toward reversals in reading and on the test of auditory discrimination. The results indicate that poor spellers have not acquired so well the habit of left to right eye movements in reading or the ability to distinguish pairs of words differing only slightly in sound. These abilities are undoubtedly due to early training in school as well as to some possible constitutional factor. The third exception was studied only incidentally in this investigation, but the importance of visual perception (which is probably partly constitutional) in distinguishing between good and poor spellers has been emphasized elsewhere. [22, 25, 33, 36, 68]

A third constitutional factor, kinaesthesis, revealed little or no difference between the normal and retarded groups. A slight tendency for the poor speller to excel in a learning method which stressed arm and hand movements is probably offset by a reliable difference in favor of the good spellers on a method which involved kinaesthetic stimuli in the form of lip and throat movements.

The slight group differences found in constitutional factors (with the exceptions noted above) do not preclude the possibility of their being an important cause of spelling disability in individual cases. Case studies on pages 36, 45, and 49 illustrate that defects of vision or hearing, in combination with other factors, may be definitely associated with spelling disability. This is also true of pupils other than those presented in the case studies. The fact that slight group differences may exist with important individual constitutional difficulties, points to (1) the necessity of individual diagnosis of spelling disabilities and (2) the importance of a more thorough examination of pupils on entering school, and at regular intervals thereafter. A more thorough physical examination would include tests of functional as well as organic factors in hearing, vision, and motor control. Some of the reading readiness tests [1] recently developed are attempts at a suitable functional measure of factors basic for spelling and other language activities. Forewarned by physiological and functional test results, the teacher can make special efforts to overcome possible constitutional handicaps, correct difficulties when they first appear, and thus lay a solid foundation for later spelling success.

In the *academic factors* tested we find the greatest number of reliable differences between the normal and retarded spelling groups (see Appendix A). The normal group reliably exceeds the

---

[1] See (A) Betts, E. A. "Ready-to-Read Tests," Meadville, Pennsylvania, Keystone View Company, 1934. (B) Hildreth, G. H. and Griffith, N.L. "Metropolitan Reading Readiness Test," Yonkers-on-Hudson, World Book Company, 1933. (C) Monroe, M. "Reading Aptitude Tests—Primary Form," Boston, Houghton Mifflin Company, 1935.

retarded group not only in written and oral spelling, but in different types of reading, quality of handwriting, pronunciation, speech rhythm, freedom from speech errors, and a number of basic skills such as giving letters for letter sounds. The evidence definitely establishes that good spelling is usually associated with abilities in a number of related language activities.

There are at least two possible explanations of this fact. The first agrees with that of Traxler [67] that there is a "general language ability." Traxler does not define such an ability. It may be thought of as a unitary mental capacity for verbal material or as a general facility in handling various language materials such as letter sounds, syllables, words, etc., in such activities as reading, writing, spelling, and speech.

Several pupils observed in this investigation may have possessed such a superior general language ability. One example was D. B., a girl whose school grade was 4.2, whose chronological age was 9–0, whose I. Q. was 117, and whose spelling grade was 6.4. Her oral spelling grade was 5.4, her pronunciation grade 5.9, her spelling of nonsense words 6.6 and 4.5. In Test 3 of the Diagnostic Battery she had one letter sound wrong, giving "e" for "i". She showed no visual or auditory difficulties. Her reading grades were 8.7 and 8.4 for general comprehension and reading for details respectively. Her rhythm score in oral reading was 5, the highest possible. Her spelling success could not be attributed to exceptional study techniques as she used the commonest varieties: pronouncing the word orally and writing it about five times each. Yet, in slightly over three minutes she learned the words "magnificent," "hippopotamus," "restaurant," and "acquaintance" and wrote them correctly when tested. This seems unusual for a girl of nine years. The examiner commented that she was "very co-operative and pleasant and likes spelling and reading best in school." A similar facility in the various types of language activities was noted in a few other pupils.

The example given, of course, does not establish the fact of a general language ability. Indeed, the second explanation, which appears the more tenable, holds that the predication of a unitary "general language ability" tends to be an over-simplification of the problem. Some support for this view is found in a preliminary report, by Thurstone, on the multiple factor analysis of mental endowment. He says, "It can easily be shown that the positive correlations among the various psychological tests can be explained in terms of a set of independent abilities, no one of which is in any sense universal or central." [67:125]

Further, although the various language abilities in this study are positively correlated, they are specialized and in certain of the cases involved they are at quite different levels in the pupils' profiles. Reading and spelling are both language arts but their coefficient of correlation is far from unity; some good readers (particularly for general comprehension) are poor spellers. Word recognition, for example, is variously related to speed and accuracy of reading, to spelling, to fluent speech, and to ability to analyze words. Certain related language techniques may underlie these abilities to handle verbal material but it seems doubtful if any central mental factor does so.

The fact that the good spellers did consistently better than the poor spellers on a series of language activities may simply mean that they have mastered a group of specific techniques which are basic to these different activities and a few of which were tested in this investigation. Such techniques might include a knowledge of letters and their sounds, ability to combine these in syllables and words, rhythm and emphasis in combining syllables, ability to analyze separate letters out of syllables, ability to note details in words and paragraphs, ability to see similarities and differences in words, a considerable meaning vocabulary, a large sight-recognition vocabulary, and related skills. These are skills, which within limits, can be acquired in the early grades by all children. The possession or lack of such a group of basic skills is probably one of the greatest factors in spelling success or disability.

Since certain skills fundamental to most spelling can be determined, it follows that (1) any diagnostic program will include a testing for these skills and (2) the school's best work will be preventive—the building up of these skills in the earlier school years.

Undoubtedly most pupils will acquire such skills in the regular course of their school career. But just as children fail occasionally to get the language skills necessary for reading [27] they may also fail to get the needed tools (probably some of the same ones) for spelling success. The important thing becomes a knowledge of the child's probable limitations (as determined by tests on entering school and observation by the teacher), the prevention if possible of linguistic failures, and the correction of difficulties as soon as they arise.

The above conclusions also point toward method in reading and spelling. It was suggested in Chapter III that the *habit* of attention to word-parts, with guidance, may transfer from certain reading methods to spelling. Modern reading methods emphasize reading for information, enjoyment, and as an aid to other school activities rather than the older synthetic, phonetic approach. The new methods have undoubtedly brought reading to a higher general level in the elementary grades than it has ever attained previously. At the same time, the prevalence of remedial reading programs indicates that under the mass education system there is always a small fraction of children who do not develop suitable word skills. The same children often suffer from spelling disabilities. The accumulated evidence seems to indicate that for the present at least, some definite training in word study is needed by most children. It would seem to be a possibility, then, that the reading period could be devoted to reading for pleasure and information and that the spelling period could be devoted to word study. For those having difficulty, this would include practice in basic skills such as those mentioned above. In addition to studying letter sounds, combining syllables, seeing similarities and differences in words, etc., the pupils would write some words, learn to spell others, know something of the interesting history of some of our English words, get special help in dictionary and library techniques, and in general acquire word skills. This work of necessity would be carefully correlated with reading, spelling, and oral and written language needs and would provide a basis for a richer variety of school and home activities.

Factors involving general *method of study* show few gross differences between the good and poor spelling groups. Analysis reveals that, instead of using the nine steps in word study advocated by Horn [42] and most spelling textbooks, both good and poor spellers use only three or four. The differences between the groups seem to lie in the fact that the retarded groups tend to use more unthinking forms of attack such as simply saying the word or spelling it orally letter by letter, while the good spellers tend to use a more active attack such as utilizing syllabication and checking the written word.

The results of the present study are not in agreement with suggestions by Lay [8] and Baird [56] that combining several methods of presentation is probably the best approach to word study, nor is there any evidence to support Horn's statement that "The methods which are suitable for the good speller are apparently also suitable for the poor speller." [42:64]

It is obvious that not all the fifteen techniques recorded in this study are suitable for all pupils learning spelling. In fact, since the successful spellers use three or four techniques that seem to work, it may be that the nine steps of study usually recommended are needlessly complex. Higley and Higley have obtained good results with a method of study which requires an accurate visual perception of the words as a necessary first step. They say of it: "Care is taken that in this first visual exposure of the word, the child is not confused by introducing auditory, or kinaesthetic impressions from the motor acts of speaking, spelling or writing a word." [37:237]

At the same time it is apparent that the members of the poor spelling group do not, as a rule, use the most effective techniques. The teaching of spelling has been unable to impose on the members of either of the groups studied, the set, formal system which prevails in most classrooms. When asked to study words as they usually do they select only three or four steps, and the chief difference seems to be that the normal spellers have acquired the most adequate steps. A reliably greater number of the normal spellers showed definite preference for a method of study which stressed one type of imagery, but there was some evidence that they varied their procedure somewhat with the form of the different words. The evidence is clear that the poor speller seldom develops an efficient attack on new words. One of the most important outcomes of the present study is its demonstration of the fact that poor spellers have not acquired adequate techniques of word study; it would seem that elementary school spelling programs should place less emphasis on acquiring a spelling vocabulary of four or five thousand words and more emphasis on developing in their pupils techniques for the mastery of new words they need to use.

The above paragraphs have included summaries and conclusions from the relationships between spelling disability and constitutional, academic-achievement, and study-method factors. For any one case it is impossible to say which of the three divisions (or their subdivisions) is most closely related to spelling difficulties —a major causal factor may lie in one division for one pupil and in an entirely different division for another. In general, the results of this study suggest that slight constitutional difficulties do not of themselves cause spelling disability but upon rare occasions major difficulties in intelligence, vision, hearing, or speech may be the outstanding causal factor. (Schonell [60] found four major speech difficulties in one hundred five cases in spelling disability.) The present investigation discovered more reliable differences between good and poor spellers in academic-achievement items than in the other two divisions (see Appendix A). Many of these academic items do not cause spelling disability but are rather associated with it. Both case study and group results suggest the importance of acquiring a group of basic word skills, which are necessary for success in reading, spelling, and other language activities. If these are not acquired in the early school years, a succession of failures and maladjustments seems almost sure to result. Probably the most important part of the school program in spelling is the discovery of possible language difficulties and the prevention of them by skilled pedagogy. At a somewhat later stage in school development the most important factors in spelling disability shift from certain academic achievements to factors of study-method or attack on new words. Systems of studying spelling are urgently needed which are less formal and ritualistic, and which place more emphasis on methods of studying new words rather than learning a prescribed list. At this later stage the possession of adequate and varied techniques of word study seems to be the best assurance of spelling success. The possession of such techniques allows for some incidental learning and the rich language experiences which are the best preventives of spelling disability.

SELECTED BIBLIOGRAPHY

1. ABBOTT, EDWINA E. "On the Analysis of Memory Consciousness in Orthography." *Psychological Review Monograph Supplement*, XI, No. 1, 1909, 127-158.

2. ABERNETHY, ETHEL M. "Photographic Eye Movements in Studying Spelling." *Journal of Educational Psychology*, XX, 1929, 695-701.

3. BETTS, E. A. *Keystone Ready to Read Tests—Manual of Directions.* Meadville, Pa., Keystone View Co., 1934. pp. 48.

4. BETTS, E. A. *The Prevention and Correction of Reading Difficulties.* Evanston, Ill., Row, Peterson and Co., 1936. pp. xiv, 402.

5. BLANCHARD, PHYLLIS. "Reading Difficulties in Relation to Difficulties of Personality and Emotional Development." *Mental Hygiene*, XX, No. 3, July 1936, 384-413.

6. BOND, GUY L. *The Auditory and Speech Characteristics of Poor Readers.* Contributions to Education, No. 657. New York, Bureau of Publications, Teachers College, Columbia University, 1935. 48 pp.

7. BOOK, WILLIAM F. "How a Special Disability in Spelling Was Diagnosed and Corrected." *Journal of Applied Psychology*, XIII, 1929, 378-393.

8. BREED, FREDERICK S. *How to Teach Spelling.* Dansville, N. Y., F. A. Owen Co., 1930. pp. viii, 177.

9. Buckingham, B. R. and Dolch, E. W. *A Combined Word List.* Boston, Ginn and Co., 1936. pp. 185.

10. CARNEY, N. "Factors in the Mental Processes of School Children." *British Journal of Psychology*, VII, 1914-15, 453-490.

11. Carmen, E. Kate. "The Cause of Chronic Bad Spelling." *Journal of Pedagogy*, 13, 1900, 86-91.

12. Carroll, Herbert A. *Generalization of Bright and Dull Children: A Comparative Study with Specific Reference to Spelling.* Contributions to Education No. 439. New York, Bureau of Publications, Teachers College, Columbia University, 1930. pp. viii. 54.

13. CATTELL, J. McKEEN. "Ueber die Zeit der Erkennung und Benennung von Schriftzeichen, Bildern und Farben." *Philos. Studien*, 1885, 635-650.

14. COLE, LUELLA. "A Successful Experiment in the Teaching of Handwriting by Analytic Methods." *Journal of Psychology*, I, 1933-36, 209-221.

15. DAVIS, GEORGIA. "Remedial Work in Spelling." *Elementary School Journal*, XXVII, April 1927, 615-626.

16. FAIRHURST, SUSIE S. "Psychological Analysis and Educational Method in Spelling." *Report of British Association for the Advancement of Science* (Eighty-Third Meeting), 1913, 302-304, 687.

17. FARRIS, L. P. *Visual Defects as Factors Influencing Achievement in Reading.* Doctor's Thesis, University of California, May 1936. pp. 157 mimeographed.

18. FENDRICK, PAUL. *Visual Characteristics of Poor Readers.* Contributions to Education No. 656. New York, Bureau of Publications, Teachers College, Columbia University, 1935. pp. 54.

19. FENDRICK, P. AND BOND, G. L. "Delinquency and Reading." *Pedagogical Seminary,* XLVIII, March 1936, 236-243.

20. FERNALD, G. W. "On Certain Language Disabilities." *Mental Measurements Monographs,* No. 11, August 1936. pp. 121.

21. FLOYD, HAZEL. *Cases of Spelling Disability: Their Diagnosis and Treatment.* Unpublished Master's Thesis, Department of Education, University of Chicago, 1927. pp. 222.

22. FORAN, THOMAS G. *The Psychology and Teaching of Spelling.* Washington, D. C., Catholic Education Press, 1934. pp. xi, 234.

23. GATES, ARTHUR I. "A Modern Systematic versus an Opportunistic Method of Teaching." *Teachers College Record,* XXVII, 1926, 679-700.

24. GATES, ARTHUR I. "An Experimental Comparison of the Study-Test and Test-Study Methods in Spelling." *Journal of Educational Psychology,* XXII, 1931, 1-19.

25. GATES, ARTHUR I. "A Study of the Role of Visual Perception, Intelligence and Certain Associative Processes in Reading and Spelling." *Journal of Educational Psychology,* XVII, 1926, 433-445.

26. GATES, ARTHUR I. *Manual of Directions for Gates Silent Reading Tests, Grades 3 to 8.* New York, Bureau of Publications, Teachers College, Columbia University, revised edition 1934.

27. GATES, ARTHUR I. *The Improvement of Reading.* New York, The Macmillan Co., 1935. pp. xvi, 668.

28. GATES, ARTHUR I. *The Psychology of Reading and Spelling with Special Reference to Disability.* Contributions to Education No. 129. New York, Bureau of Publications, Teachers College, Columbia University, 1922. pp. 108.

29. GATES, ARTHUR I. "The Psychological Basis of Remedial Reading." *The Educational Record,* 17, Supplement 10, October 1936, 109-123.

30. GATES, A. I. AND BOND, G. L. "Reliability of Telebinocular Tests of Beginning Pupils." *Journal of Educational Psychology,* January 1937, 31-36.

31. GATES, A. I. AND CHASE, E. H. "Methods and Theories of Learning to Spell Tested by Studies of Deaf Children." *Journal of Educational Psychology,* XVII, 1926, 289-300.

32. GILBERT, LUTHER C. "An Experimental Investigation of Eye Movements in Learning to Spell Words." *Psychological Monographs,* XLIII No. 3, 1932. pp. 81.

33. GILBERT, LUTHER C. "Experimental Investigation of a Flash-Card Method of Teaching Spelling." *Elementary School Journal,* XXXII, 1932, 337-351.

34. GILL, EDMUND J. "The Teaching of Spelling." *Journal of Experimental Pedagogy,* I, 1912, 310-319.

35. HANSBURG, HENRY. *Some Educational and Psychological Influences of the Print Shop in the Elementary School.* Unpublished study. 171 pp. mss.

36. HARTMANN, GEORGE W. "The Relative Influence of Visual and Auditory Factors in Spelling Ability." *Journal of Educational Psychology,* XXII, 1931, 371-381.

37. HIGLEY, B. R. AND B. M. "An Effective Method of Learning to Spell." *Educational Research Bulletin*, XV, No. 9, Columbus, Ohio State University, December 16, 1936, 235-242.

38. HILDERBRANDT, EDITH L. "The Psychological Analysis of Spelling." *Pedagogical Seminary*, 30, 1923, 371-381.

39. HOLLINGWORTH, LETA S. "The Psychological Examination of Poor Spellers." *Teachers College Record*, XX, March 1919, 126-132.

40. HOLLINGWORTH, LETA S. *The Psychology of Special Disability in Spelling*. Contributions to Education No. 88. New York, Bureau of Publications, Teachers College, Columbia University, 1918. pp. vi, 105.

41. HORN, ERNEST. "Curriculum Investigations at the Elementary and Secondary School Levels: Spelling." *Review of Educational Research*, IV, No. 2, 1934, 143-146.

42. HORN, ERNEST. "Principles of Teaching Spelling as Derived from Scientific Investigation." *National Society for the Study of Education 18th Year book*, Part II. Bloomington, Ill., Public School Publishing Co., 1919, 52-77.

43. HOUSER, J. D. "The Relation of Spelling Ability to General Intelligence and to Meaning Vocabulary." *Elementary School Journal*, XVI, 1915, 190-199.

44. JAVAL, E. "Sur la physiologie de la lecture." *Annales d'Oculistique*, 1878.

45. KAY, MARJORIE E. "The Effect of Errors in Pronunciation on Spelling." *Elementary English Review*, VII, 1930, 64-66.

46. KIEFER, F. A. AND SANGREN, P. V. "An Experimental Investigation of the Causes of Poor Spelling Among University Students with Suggestions for Improvement." *Journal of Educational Psychology*, XVI, 1925, 38-47.

47. LOUTTIT, C. M. *Clinical Psychology*. New York, Harper and Brothers, 1936. pp. xv, 695.

48. McGOVNEY, MARGARITA. "Spelling Deficiency in Children of Superior General Ability." *Elementary English Review*, VII, 1930, 146-148.

49. McKEE, PAUL. "Teaching Spelling by Column and Context Forms." *Journal of Educational Research*, XV, 1927, 246-255; 339-348.

50. MENDENHALL, J. E. "An Analysis of Spelling Errors. New York, Bureau of Publications, Teachers College, Columbia University, 1930. pp. 65.

51. *Modern School Achievement Tests: Manual of Directions*. New York, Bureau of Publications, Teachers College, Columbia University.

52. MORT, P. R. AND GATES, A. I. *The Acceptable Uses of Achievement Tests*. New York, Bureau of Publications, Teachers College, Columbia University, 1932. pp. 85.

53. ORTON, S. T. *Reading, Writing and Speech Problems in Children*. New York, W. W. Norton and Co., 1937. pp. 215.

54. PHILLIPS, W. C. AND ROWELL, H. G. *Your Hearing: How to Preserve and Aid It*. New York, D. Appleton and Co., 1932. pp. xiii, 232.

55. PRESSEY, LUELLA C. "An Investigation into the Elements of Ability to Spell." Ohio State University, *Educational Research Bulletin*, May 1927, 203-204.

56. PRYOR, H. C. AND PITTMAN, M. S. *A Guide to the Teaching of Spelling*. New York, The Macmillan Co., 1921. pp. 141.

57. *Review of Educational Research*, I, No. 4. "Special Methods in the Elementary School Subjects III, Spelling," October 1931.

58. ROBACK, A. A. "Writing Slips and Personality." *Character and Personality,* I, 1932, 137-146.

59. SCHONELL, FREDERICK J. "Ability and Disability in Spelling among Educated Adults." *British Journal of Educational Psychology,* VI, 1936, 123-146.

60. SCHONELL, FREDERICK J. "Relation between Defective Speech and Disability in Spelling." *British Journal of Educational Psychology,* IV, 1934, 123-139.

61. SELZER, CHARLES A. *Lateral Dominance and Visual Fusion: Their Applications to Difficulties in Reading, Writing, Spelling and Speech.* Harvard Monographs in Education, No. 12. Cambridge, Mass., Harvard University Press, 1933. pp. 119.

62. STARCH, DANIEL. *Educational Psychology.* Chapter XIX, Spelling. New York, The Macmillan Co., 1929. pp. 374-408.

63. SUDWEEKS, JOSEPH. "Practical Helps in Teaching Spelling: Summary of Helpful Principles and Methods." *Journal of Educational Research,* XVI, 1927, 106-118.

64. THOMPSON, ROBERT S. *The Effectiveness of Modern Spelling Instruction.* Contributions to Education No. 436. New York, Bureau of Publications, Teachers College, Columbia University, 1930. pp. 81.

65. THORNDIKE, E. L. "The Thorndike Scale for Handwriting of Children." Reprinted from the monograph *Handwriting.* New York, Bureau of Publications, Teachers College, Columbia University, 1912.

66. THURSTONE, L. L. "A New Concept of Intelligence and a New Method of Measuring Primary Abilities." *The Educational Record,* Supplement 10, October 1936, 124-138.

67. TRAXLER, A. E. *The Use of Test Results in Diagnosis and Instruction in the Tool Subjects.* Educational Records Bulletin No. 18. New York, Educational Records Bureau, October 1936. pp. 74.

68. VISITATION, SISTER MARY OF THE. "Visual Perception in Reading and Spelling: A Statistical Analysis." Washington, D. C., Catholic University of America, *Educational Research Bulletin,* IV No. 1, 1929. pp. 48.

69. WATSON, ALICE E. *Experimental Studies in the Psychology and Pedagogy of Spelling.* Contributions to Education No. 638. New York, Bureau of Publications, Teachers College, Columbia University, 1935. pp. 144.

70. WINCH, W. H. "Experimental Researches on Learning to Spell." *Journal of Educational Psychology,* IV, 1913, 525-537; 579-592.

71. WINCH, W. H. "Further Experimental Researches on Learning to Spell." *Journal of Educational Psychology,* V, 1914, 449-460.

72. WYCKOFF, A. E. "Constitutional Bad Spellers." *Pedagogical Seminary,* II, 1892, 448-50.

APPENDIX A

SUMMARY OF STATISTICAL COMPARISONS BETWEEN NORMAL AND RETARDED SPELLERS

A. SUMMARY OF THE FACTORS ON WHICH NORMAL SPELLERS RELIABLY EXCEEDED RETARDED SPELLERS

No.	Test	Description	D(N–R)	C.R. σ
A. Constitutional Factors				
1	Diag. Batt. 8	No. correct responses—Auditory Discrimination	1.20	4.3
2		Attitude to spelling—Per Cent rated Good, Likes, etc.	29.0	3.7
B. Academic Achievements				
3	Diag. Batt. 2	Word Pronunciation—Grade Score	1.55	22.1
4	Diag. Batt. 1	Oral Spelling—Grade Score	1.24	13.8
5	Diag. Batt. 5	Spelling Nonsense Word of Two Syllables—Grade Score	2.22	10.6
6	Gates 3 to 8	Reading Grade—Type A, General Comprehension	1.78	8.9
7	Gates 3 to 8	Speed by Paragraphs, Type A	4.36	7.7
8		Recorded Oral Reading—Rhythm	1.09	7.6
9	Thorndike Scale	Quality of Handwriting	.73	7.3
10	Gates 3 to 8	Reading Grade, Type D, Note Details	1.31	7.3
11	Gates 3 to 8	Speed by Questions Answered, Type D	8.23	6.4
12	Gates 3 to 8	Reading Accuracy, Type D, Per Cent	20.34	6.3
13	Gates 3 to 8	Reading Accuracy, Type A, Per Cent	21.11	5.9
14	Diag. Batt. 4	Spelling One Nonsense Syllable—Grade Score	1.36	5.5
15	Diag. Batt. 3	Giving Letters for Letter Sounds—Grade Score	.81	5.1
C. Methods of Studying Spelling				
16	Diag. Batt. 2	Method in Pronunciation—Per Cent Blending Good	53.0	7.7
17	Diag. Batt. 2	Pronunciation—Analyses by Syllables—Per Cent	43.0	5.6
18	Diag. Batt. 7	No. Words Correct, studied "auditorily"	.76	4.8
19	Diag. Batt. 7	No. Words Correct—Three Methods	.77	4.5

B. Summary of the Factors on Which Normal Spellers Exceeded Retarded Spellers, but not Reliably So

No.	Test	Description	D(N–R)	C.R.σ
A. Constitutional Factors				
1	Audiometer	Total Range Per Cent Hearing Loss for Best Ear	.68	1.19
2	Audiometer	Speech Range Per Cent Hearing Loss for Best Ear	.45	.85
3	Betts	Per Cent Passing Far-Point Fusion Test	6.6	.81
B. Academic Achievements				
4	Mod. Sch. Ach.	Type of Error in 20 Words—Per Cent Phonetic Errors	1.7	2.2
5	Mod. Sch. Ach.	Type of Error in 20 Words—Per Cent Omissions	2.8	1.8
6	Mod. Sch. Ach.	Type of Error in 20 Words—Per Cent Transpositions	1.0	1.4
7	Thorndike Scale	Speed of Handwriting—letters per minute	2.24	.99
8	Speech Record	Number of Vowel Errors	.05	.15
9	Mod. Sch. Ach.	Type of Error in 20 Words—Per Cent Insertions	.1	.10
C. Methods of Studying Spelling				
10	Diag. Batt. 9	Per Cent Stated as Excelling in "Auditory" Method	15.0	2.5
11	Diag. Batt. 7	Per Cent Frequency of Use of Technique 8*	4.0	2.5
12	Diag. Batt. 9	Per Cent Stated as Excelling in "Visual" Method	16.0	2.4
13	Diag. Batt. 7	Per Cent Frequency of Use of Technique 11–1	3.0	2.3
14	Diag. Batt. 1	Per Cent Using Method in Oral Spelling—Phonetically	8.0	2.3
15	Diag. Batt. 7	No. Words Correct Studied "Visually"	.35	2.1
16	Diag. Batt. 7	Per Cent Frequency of Use of Technique 4	1.0	1.8
17	Diag. Batt. 7	Per Cent Frequency of Use of Technique 12	2.0	1.7
18	Diag. Batt. 1	Per Cent Using Method in Oral Spelling—by Syllables	8.0	1.6
19	Diag. Batt. 7	Per Cent Frequency of Use of Technique 9	10.0	1.3
20	Diag. Batt. 7	No. Words Correct Studied "Kinaesthetically"	.15	1.1
21	Diag. Batt. 7	Per Cent Frequency of Use of Technique 2	1.0	.91
22	Diag. Batt. 7	Per Cent Frequency of Use of Technique 11	1.0	.77
23	Diag. Batt. 7	Time in Seconds Studying Four Words	13.6	.44
24	Diag. Batt. 1	Per Cent of Use in Oral Spelling—Sp. Word as a Unit	2.0	.38
25	Diag. Batt. 7	Number of Efforts Used in Study	.03	.03

* For explanation of numbers of techniques see Table 13, page 71.

C. Summary of Factors on Which Normal and Retarded Spellers Had Identical Mean Scores

No.	Test	Description	D(N–R)	C.R.σ
A. Constitutional				
1	Betts	Per Cent Passing Vertical Imbalance	o	
2	Betts	Per Cent Passing Ametropia—Left Eye at 13 Inches	o	
3	Betts	Per Cent Passing Ametropia—Left Eye at infinite distance	o	
4	Betts	Per Cent Passing Ametropia—Right Eye at infinite distance	o	
C. Methods of Studying Spelling				
5	Diag. Batt. 7	Number of Study Techniques Used per Word	o	
6	Diag. Batt. 7	Per Cent Frequency of Use of Technique 3	o	
7	Diag. Batt. 7	Per Cent Frequency of Use of Technique 6	o	
8	Diag. Batt. 7	Per Cent Frequency of Use of Technique 7	o	
9	Diag. Batt. 7	Per Cent Frequency of Use of Technique 12–1	o	

D. Summary of Factors on Which Retarded Spellers Exceeded Normal Spellers but not Reliably So

No.	Test	Description	D(R–N)	C.R.σ
A. Constitutional				
1	Betts	Per Cent Passing Ametropia, Right Eye, at 80 in.	1.3	.19
2	Betts	Per Cent Passing Ametropia, Left Eye, at 80 in.	1.7	.20
3	Betts	Per Cent Passing Ametropia, Right Eye, at 13 in.	1.6	.24
4	Betts	Per Cent Passing Visual Acuity Right Eye	1.6	.33
5	Betts	Per Cent Passing Stereopsis	4.9	.78
6	Betts	Per Cent Passing Far-Point Lateral Imbalance	4.9	.79
7	Betts	Per Cent Passing Visual Acuity Left Eye	5.0	.85
8	Betts	Per Cent Passing Visual Acuity Both Eyes	4.9	1.2
9	Betts	Attitude to Spelling, Per Cent Rated "Fair," etc.	10.0	1.45
10	Betts	Per Cent Passing Near Point Fusion	13.1	1.5
11	Betts	Per Cent Passing Near Point Lateral Imbalance	19.7	2.5
12	Betts	Attitude to Spelling—Per Cent Rated "Poor," etc.	19.	2.97

D. Summary of Factors on Which Retarded Spellers Exceeded Normal Spellers but not Reliably So (*Continued*)

No.	Test	Description	D(R–N)	C.R.$_\sigma$
B. Academic Achievement				
13	Mod. Sch. Ach.	Type of Error in 20 Words—Substitutions	2.8	1.8
14	Speech Record	Number of Errors—Omissions	1.4	2.3
15	Speech Record	Number of Wrong Articulations in Key Words	.94	2.7
16	Speech Record	Number of Consonant Errors	2.4	2.7
17	Speech Record	Number of Errors—Substitutions	2.6	2.95
C. Methods of Studying Spelling				
18	Diag. Batt. 9	Per Cent Stated as Excelling in "Kinaesthetic"	1.0	.20
19	Diag. Batt. 2	Pronunciation—Per Cent Blending Rated "Fair"	4.0	.51
20	Diag. Batt. 1	Method in Oral Spelling—Per Cent by Digraphs	4.0	.63
21	Diag. Batt. 2	Method in Analyzing by Sound Units—Oral Spelling	8.0	1.3
22	Diag. Batt. 7	Method in Frequency of Use of Technique 10–1	3.0	1.5
23	Diag. Batt. 7	Method in Frequency of Use of Technique 10	4.0	2.5

E. Summary of Factors on Which Retarded Spellers Reliably Exceeded Normal Spellers

No.	Test	Description	D(R–N)	C.R.$_\sigma$
B. Academic Achievement				
1	Mod. Sch. Ach.	Type of Error in 20 Words—Per Cent Additions	2.6	3.3
2	Speech Record	Total Errors—Additions, Insertions, etc.	4.12	3.6
3	Speech Record	Total Mispronunciations Outside Key Words	4.28	4.3
C. Methods of Studying Spelling				
4	Diag. Batt. 1	Method in Oral Spelling—Per Cent Using Letter by Letter	15.0	3.1
5	Diag. Batt. 7	Per Cent Frequency of Use of Technique 1	7.0	3.2
6	Diag. Batt. 2	Pronunciation—Per Cent Guesses Word as a Whole	35.0	4.7
7	Diag. Batt. 2	Pronunciation—Per Cent Rated "Poor" in Blending	57.6	9.6

APPENDIX B

DIRECTIONS FOR ADMINISTERING AND SCORING DIAGNOSTIC TEST SERIES

Test. 1. *Spelling Words Orally (Gates B4)*

After the child is at ease say, "I am going to say a word. Then I want you to say it after me and to spell it for me. Do you understand? The first word is *me*. Will you say that and spell it for me?" Record by plus (+) if word is correct. Indicate misspelling and method of spelling thus: prison, if no division between the letters; p-r-i-s-n for letter by letter; pr-pri-pris-n, etc. Number the errors (1), (2), etc. and stop at ten errors. *Score:* Number correct the first attempt (allow an instant correction). Before giving Test 2 write in comments. Summary may be checked here or at end of complete test. For method of scoring omissions etc., see scoring tables.

Test 2. *Word Pronunciation*

If word is correctly pronounced make no mark, unless phonetic methods were employed. If child fails on first trial, (*a*) write in his pronunciation above the word; (*b*) ask pupil to try again. If child fails on the second trial, (*a*) draw a line through the word; (*b*) give no credit for third trial. If child says, "I don't know the word," encourage him to try it. Phonetic analysis and blending are allowable if the child can use them. If he will not try draw a line through the word. Continue until the child misses ten consecutive words and indicate clearly the kind of mispronunciation. It is often necessary to attempt to speed up this test. *Score:* Word correct first trial, score 2; word correct second trial, score 1. Total the points. Summary may be completed at end of the complete test. For scoring transpositions, etc., see scoring tables.

Test. 3. *Giving Letters for Letter Sounds (Gates B1)*

Examiner says, "I am going to give you the sound of a letter and I want you to tell me what letter that sound stands for. What letter stands for the sound "s" (hiss). Similarly for other sounds. *Note:* Sound "i" as in *it;* "oo" as in *root;* "g" as in *get.* Give a second chance if necessary; if correct, give half credit. *Score:* The following are correct: for "s," *s* or *c;* for "oo," either *oo, o,* or *u;* for "k" either *k* or *c.* All other variations are wrong. Score is number right.

Test 4. *Spelling One Syllable (Gates B2)*

Say, "I am going to say a word that may not be a real word and I want you to spell it for me in the best way. How do you spell 'ub'?" Etc. Write in the incorrect spellings.

Syllable	Pronounce as in	Credit of 1 Point	Credit of ½ Point
1. ub	tub	ub	ob, oub, ube
2. ip	tip	ip, hip	eip, ipe
3. tie	necktie	tie, ti, ty, tye	tuy
4. sot	rhyme with hot	sot, sote	sat

Syllable	Pronounce as in	Credit of 1 Point	Credit of ½ Point
5. gib	g as in get; ib as in bib	gib	geb, gibe
6. zar	sounded as Czar	zar, sar	zor, shar, shar
7. nuk	uk as in fluke	nuk, nook, knuk, knock	noc, nok, knok, nock
8. arp	harp	arp	orp, arep
9. eck	neck	eck, ek, ec	eack, eak, ekk, wek
10. mip	ip as in tip	mip	mep

Test 5. *Spelling Two Syllables (Gates B3)*

Say, "I am going to say some more words that may not be real words and I want you to spell them for me as well as you can. How do you spell 'nubit'?" Etc. Write in the incorrect spellings.

Word	Pronunciation	Credit of 1 Point	Credit ½ Point
1. nubit	Long u and short i	nubit, nubbit, (k)newbit	nubeit, nobit, newbet nubet, nobbit, newbid
2. argos	ar as in are; go as in going	argos, argose, aregos(e)	argoos, argues, argeos, arges
3. sopot	so and pot like Eng.	sopot, sopat, soappat, sewpot, soapot, soapat	soppoat, soupot
4. urfo	ur as in fur; fo as in four	erfo(e), urfo, irfo(e) urpho	urfol, erful, earfo, urful, arfo, irfol
5. piptuk	short i; tuk as tuck	piptuk, piptuck, piptuc, piptoc, piptock, piptok	peptuck, peptock, peptuc, peptuk, peptok, peptoc
6. zignuk	zig as zig-zag; u is long	(s)zignuk, (s)zignook, (s)zignuke, (s)zignok	
7. iptie	ip as in tip; tie as in necktie	iptie, ipti, ipty, hiptie	eiptie, iptui
8. ubzar	ub as in tub; zar as Czar	ubzar, ubzhar, ubsar	ubsor, ubzor, obsar, upzar, obzar

Checking may be done at end of complete test. Comments should be written in before giving Test 6.

Test 6. *Word Reversals (Gates VIII 1)*

Hold up card containing several words. Say, "I would like you to read these words for me straight across the page. Go ahead." If words are correctly pronounced, leave unmarked. Consider *only the first response* and write down a mistake above the word.

If child attempts a phonetic translation of the word, encourage him to continue until he says a word. *Score:* Total the number of wrong words. Total the number of words showing full or partial reversals. Find the percentage which the reversals are of the total number of errors.

Test 7. *Spelling Attack*

Select on the cards the last four of the words wrong in Test 1 (numbered 7, 8, 9, 10). Say, "Now we are going to study some words that were hard for you on the first try. I have picked out on these cards the words that you had wrong then. Now I want you to study these words very carefully so that you will be *sure* to have them *all correct* when I ask you to spell them again. In studying the word you may do anything you wish, such as saying it, writing it with pencil and paper, looking at it; just do the things that you usually do when you are studying a new word. The only difference is that I want you to say out loud what you are *thinking* so that I, too, will know what you are doing. Do you understand? All right, study the words the way you usually do, but say out loud what you are doing. Are you ready? The first word is .... (pointing to it on card). How do you say the word? Yes, that is right. Now tell me all you are doing as you carefully study the word."

Have pencil and paper before the child so he can write if he wishes. Record exactly what he says and does in studying the word; record the *time* spent on each word. Finish checking his attack on one word (by numbers) before giving the second, etc. When the four words have been studied have the pupil write them in the space provided after the examiner has covered his notes above. Dictate the words in this order: 2, 4, 1, 3.

Test 8. *Auditory Discrimination*

Have the pupil read the mixed list of words (separate sheet) to be sure he recognizes all. If he makes any mistakes correct them at once and check again after the complete list has been read. Then place the child about six feet away with his back to the examiner, looking at paired words.

Say, "You are looking at pairs of words that sound alike. Starting at the first pair and going on to the next in order, I am going to say one, and only one, of the words in each pair. I want you to draw a line under the *one* word that I say in each pair. Do you understand? The first word is *by;* the next word is *do; are; dim; bay; big; shell; weather; ceiling; fountain; tied; sheer; slave; ferry; where.*"

Pronounce words in ordinary tone, without haste. Allow interval for pupil to mark, but do not repeat a word. Score: Total number of correct identifications.

(Rest the pupil before giving the next test.)

Test 9. *Visual, Auditory, and Kinaesthetic Spelling (Order Changes Each Time)*

Have paper, pencil, and manilla folder ready. Check order in which words should be studied this time: (*a*) Visual, Auditory, Kinaesthetic; (*b*) Auditory, Kinaesthetic, Visual; (*c*) Kinaesthetic, Visual, Auditory. Indicate the order of the methods used in the blanks provided in the text booklet. Then select the fourth, fifth, and sixth words the pupil had wrong on Test 1. Match them on the accompanying sheet of words matched for difficulty. The pupil studies three words by each of the methods: visual, auditory, and kinaesthetic (but not necessarily in that order). In the tests below the child should see only one word at a time, the one being studied. Words that have been studied may be folded under with the top of the sheet of paper used.

Visual. Write the first of the three words near the top of a sheet of paper. Say, "Look at this word carefully and then pronounce it." Help pupil on pronunciation if necessary. Say, "I want you to study this word by looking at it very carefully. Look for the hard parts of the word and remember them. When you think you can write the word, cover it with your left hand and write it." Pupil does so. Say, "Compare your word carefully with the other. Is it right?" If correct, ask the pupil to write it once again after looking, and compare. If the word is not correct, ask the child to continue looking and writing until the word is correct on two successive trials. After the pupil has it correct twice in succession, say, "You may practice the word more if you wish, or we can go on to the next one if you are ready." Write the second word on the sheet of paper, study as before. Repeat for the three words. Comment on pupil's reactions in space provided before going on to Auditory Method below.

Auditory. The examiner writes the word at the top of a new sheet of paper. Say, "Here is the next word to be studied differently. I am going to say a word and then I want you to say it after me. Then I want you to use it in a sentence. Now say .... and use it in a sentence." Examiner gives an easy descriptive sentence if child cannot. After covering the word say, "Now I am going to spell the word and I want you to spell it after me." Say the word and spell it. Continue until pupil says word and spells it correctly after examiner twice in succession, leaving about 5 seconds between trials. If the pupil wishes to spell the second trial immediately after the first, say, "Now rest just a moment." Tell the pupil he may spell the word to himself oftener if he wishes. If pupil has difficulty in spelling word, correct as soon as mistake is made, re-spell, and emphasize part to be corrected. Comment on pupil's reactions in space provided before going on to Kinaesthetic Method.

Kinaesthetic. Say, "Now we are going to study some words by writing them and not looking at what we have written. I am going to cover your hand and the paper with this cardboard so that you cannot see what you have written." Examiner writes the first word on sheet of paper. Say, "Here is the first word, ... (pronouncing it). Write the word as often as you like without saying the letters to yourself or without seeing how you have written it. Practice writing the word until you are sure that you have it right at least twice and try to get the *feeling* of the word as you write it."

Pupil practices with writing hand covered by manilla folder. When he is sure he knows the word (examiner checks to see it is correct twice in succession), examiner writes the next word for him and repeats the above. The pupil may see, one at a time, the words the examiner has written for him, but is not to see how he writes the word himself. The two correct trials should be without seeing the word the examiner has written. Fill in comments under Kinaesthetic.

Note: The order of the above will be changed as indicated above for each examination. The nine words will then be dictated in the following order: 2, 5, 8, 3, 6, 9, 1, 4, 7. Fill in final comments on this test comparing pupil's reactions to the various means of study—amount of hesitation, number of trials on different words, apparent likes or dislikes, whether or not the child seems to be strongly visual, auditory, or kinaesthetic; in case of errors, summarize the kinds on the final test and how they were related to the study procedure.

Matched Words Used in Test 9 Diagnostic Battery:

1.	me	at	to
2.	it	go	he
3.	do	in	be
4.	but	and	cap
5.	are	can	get
6.	day	cow	hot
7.	nine	wife	cool
8.	card	most	fine
9.	mail	held	post
10.	catch	other	field

11.	teach	empty	since
12.	built	noise	laugh
13.	afraid	enough	minute
14.	travel	golden	beside
15.	prison	barrel	really
16.	factory	advance	subject
17.	visitor	exhibit	traffic
18.	measure	neither	soldier
19.	marriage	familiar	ambition
20.	circular	response	guardian
21.	estimate	decision	quantity
22.	elaborate	technical	procedure
23.	amusement	immediate	desirable
24.	necessary	therefore	excellent
25.	difficulty	commission	throughout
26.	approaches	attentions	accomplish
27.	restaurant	surrenders	perfection
28.	arrangement	experiments	contributes
29.	information	imagination	disappoints
30.	magnificent	brilliantly	discoveries
31.	acquaintance	transferring	accommodates
32.	hippopotamus		
33.	architecture		
34.	extraordinary		
35.	miscellaneous		
36.	conscientious		

GATES–RUSSELL SPELLING DIAGNOSIS TESTS

Name..Age............I.Q. ....Grade............................

Examiner...School...Date...

Language parents speak   (a) to one another....................................(b) to children...................................

To the Examiner:

This booklet contains tests fully described in Gates and Russell, *Diagnostic and Remedial Spelling Manual* (Bureau of Publications, Teachers College). The subject and the examiner must both be provided with booklets. They should exchange them for certain tests so that the written records of both subject and examiner may be contained in one booklet.

TEST	RAW SCORE	GRADE SCORE
1. Spelling Words Orally		
2. Word Pronunciation		
3. Giving Letters for Letter Sounds		
4. Spelling One Syllable		
5. Spelling Two Syllables		
6. Word Reversals		
7. Spelling Attack		
8. Auditory Discrimination		
9. Visual, Auditory, Kinaesthetic and Combined Study Methods		

SUPPLEMENTARY DIAGNOSIS

Grade Score

1. Standard Test—Written Spelling ....

2. Standard Test—Silent Reading ....

3. Standard Test—Oral Reading ....

4. Vocabulary Test ....

5. Memory for Numbers ....

6. Memory for Words ....

7. Handwriting—Speed................letters per minute.

8. Handwriting—Quality...............

9. Vision Test Comments:

10. Hearing Loss. Left............%, Right............%.

11. Handedness. Comments:

12. Eyedness. Comments:

13. Speech. Comments:

14. Forming of Derivatives. Comments:

15. Use of Homonyms. Comments:

BUREAU OF PUBLICATIONS, TEACHERS COLLEGE
COLUMBIA UNIVERSITY, NEW YORK
Copyright, 1937, by Teachers College
2.10.37

1. Spelling Words (Do not ask pupil to spell any words after a total of ten errors; write errors above words spelled)

me	it	do	but	are	day
nine	card	mail	catch	teach	built
afraid	travel	prison	factory	visitor	measure
marriage	circular	estimate	elaborate	amusement	necessary
difficulty	approaches	restaurant	arrangement	information	magnificent
acquaintance	hippopotamus	architecture	extraordinary	miscellaneous	conscientious

Notes on Test 1. Score...........
Check:
...........1. Spells as a unit (prisn)   ....4. Spells by syllables (fac-try)
...........2. Spells letter by letter (m-e-s-u-r)   ....5. Spells phonetically (vizater)
...........3. Spells by digraphs (a-fr-ai-d)
Underline:
   6. Consistent in the above: yes, fairly, no.
   7. He adds syllables; omits syllables.
   8. In ten words, no. letters inserted...........; no. letters added...........   no. transpositions...........
                    no. letters omitted...........; no. substitutions...........(f for v; wh for w, etc.)

Comments:

2. Word Pronunciation

so	an	do	go	at
the	did	hen	may	son
king	door	came	late	east
every	after	child	blind	climb
window	bridge	scratch	plaster	servant
passenger	eighty	shepherd	chocolate	citizen
dispute	continue	brilliant	brightness	guardian
intelligent	impatient	temperature	profitable	reverence
irregular	manufacture	unnecessary	community	intelligence
satisfactory	countenance	preparation	affectionate	philosopher

Notes on Test 2. Score...........× 2 =...........
   1. Method: Letter by letter; sound units; by syllables; guesses word as whole (underline)
   2. Blending ability: poor, fair, good (underline)
   3. No. additions........; no. insertions........; no. omissions........; no. substitutions........; no. transpositions........
   4. Used phonetic analysis: yes, no (underline)

3. Giving Letters for Letter Sounds

     s   t   r   p   i   oo   m   f   k   g   Score...........

4. Spelling One Syllable

    ub   ip   tie   sot   gib   zar   nuk   arp   eck   mip   Score...........

5. Spelling Two Syllables

nubit   argos   sopot   urfo   piptuk   zignuk   iptie   ubzar

Notes on Test 5.   Score..................

........1. Spells as one unit   ....4. Spells by syllables
........2. Spells letter by letter
........3. Spells by digraphs   ....5. Consistent in above: yes, no, fairly.

Comments (any syllables correct in test 4 and wrong in test 5; etc.)

6. Reversals (write error above word here)

1. on	ma	bad	was	no	am	war	net	rat	now
2. raw	ton	saw	dab	won	pot	tar	saw	star	peek
3. nap	spot	dear	top	war	ma	won	team	pal	even

Complete reversals................Partial.............Total................

Total errors...............

% reversals........ ....

7. Learning to Spell Hard Words (last 4 of 10 words wrong in Test 1)

1..Time......................seconds

        (word)

Comments:

l after letter means looking at original word: use 10 *l*, etc.).

Check:
1. Pronounces correctly
2. Eyes move over word several times
3. Closes eyes to recall appearance
4. Looks at word, saying clearly
5. Fixes on hard part
6. Eyes closed a second time

7. Writes looking at word
8. Writes without looking at word
9. Writes word twice or more
10. Spells orally letter by letter
11. Spells orally by syllables
12. Spells orally by digraphs

2..Time......................seconds

      (Use numbers as above)

Comments:

3..Time............ ....seconds

      (Numbers)

Comments:

4..Time......................seconds

      (Numbers)

Comments:

Pupil's Written Words

Score..................

8.

(The pupil reads orally the following words before taking test 8. The examiner should be sure he recognizes all the words—repeat if necessary).

do; are; seeing; where; shall; wetter; tired; ferry; dim; pay; big; fountain; air; to; by; slave; cheer; bib; bay; shell; weather; shave; very; were; sheer; dim; be; tied; ceiling; mountain.

Auditory Discrimination (6 feet, back turned)

be - by   do - to   are - air   dim - din   pay - bay   bib - big
shall - shell   weather - wetter   ceiling - seeing   mountain - fountain
tied - tired   cheer - sheer   shave - slave   very - ferry   where - were

Score.....................

9. Visual, Auditory, and Kinaesthetic Spelling

Words studied *Visually*   Pupil's Final Spelling:

1.   1.
2.   2.
3.   3.
Comments: 4.
                                            5.
Words studied *Auditorily*   6.
1.   7.
2.   8.
3.   9.
Comments: 10.
                                            11.
Words studied *Kinaesthetically*   12.
1.
2.
3.
Comments:

Words studied—*Combined Method*
1.
2.
3.   Summary Test 9.   No. Correct

Comments:

V.	A.	K.	C.

Final Comments: Test 9.